Teacher education as
transformation

**Books are to be returned on or before
the last date below.**

Developing Teachers and Teaching

Series Editor: **Christopher Day**, Reader in Education Management and Director of Advanced Post-Graduate Courses in the School of Education, University of Nottingham.

Teachers and schools will wish not only to survive but also to flourish in a period which holds increased opportunities for self-management – albeit within centrally designed guidelines – combined with increased public and professional accountability. Each of the authors in this series provides perspectives which will both challenge and support practitioners at all levels who wish to extend their critical skills, qualities and knowledge of schools, pupils and teachers.

Current titles:

Angela Anning: *The First Years at School*
Les Bell and Chris Day (eds): *Managing the Professional Development of Teachers*
Joan Dean: *Professional Development in School*
C. T. Patrick Diamond: *Teacher Education as Transformation*
John Elliott: *Action Research for Educational Change*

Teacher education as transformation

A psychological perspective

C. T. Patrick Diamond

Open University Press
Milton Keynes · Philadelphia

Open University Press
Celtic Court
22 Ballmoor
Buckingham
MK18 1XW

and
1900 Frost Road, Suite 101
Bristol, PA 19007, USA

First Published 1991

British Library Cataloguing in Publication Data

Diamond, C. T. Patrick
  Teacher education as transformation: a psychological perspective. –
  (Professional learning and change series).
  1. Teachers. Professional education
  I. Title II. Series
  370.71

  ISBN 0-335-09255-1 (hb)
  ISBN 0-335-09254-3 (pbk)

Library of Congress Cataloging-in-Publication Data

Diamond, C. T. Patrick.
    Teacher education as transformation: a psychological perspective
    C. T. Patrick Diamond.
       p.   cm.—(Professional learning and change series)
    Includes bibliographical references (p.   ) and index.
    ISBN 0-335-09255-1 — ISBN 0-335-09254-3 (pbk.)
    1. Teachers—Training of. 2. Teachers—In-service training.
  3. Teachers—Self-rating of. 4. Teachers—Psychology. I. Title.
  II. Series.
  LB1707.D53   1991
  370'.71—dc20   90-45610
                                                         CIP

Typeset by Rowland Phototypesetting Ltd
Bury St Edmunds, Suffolk
Printed in Great Britain by Biddles Ltd
Guildford and King's Lynn

Dedicated to Don Bannister,
Norma, Maureen, John, Christine, Anne, Craig,
Bill and Brenda

Contents

List of figures and tables

Series editor's introduction

This book is a testament to those who believe that the major challenge for all who are involved in the professional development of teachers – whether in initial or in-service training – lies in providing the means by which they may become more critically aware of their own values, thinking and practices and thus empowering them to find new ways of teaching. Pat Diamond views teachers as essentially self-directing and self-determining but, citing examples from Australia, England and North America, he sees them as being under threat from forces of production and accountability that have 'seized the political and moral initiative' with calls for a more prescriptive education curriculum, more 'value for money' and quality control. However, this book, which is full of practical suggestions for teacher educators and teachers themselves, suggests ways in which teachers may 'release themselves from the paralysis of being hurried and harried'.

Pat Diamond's own perspective of teacher education as transformation (rather than, for example, reproduction) is derived from and extends personal construct psychology. Essentially, this places the intending teacher or teacher at the centre of his or her own learning, acknowledging the crucial role played by critical reflectivity and perspectivity leading to 'emancipatory' knowledge. In this sense, Diamond's intentions have much in common with those of John Elliott, also in this series, although the routes differ.

Pat Diamond has written a book that is international in flavour, and which provides a much needed contribution to the further development of client-centred transformational teacher education.

Christopher Day

Preface

Man has weav'd out a net and his net throwne
Upon the Heavens, and now they are his owne.
                                    John Donne

As the challenging ideas of individuals and communities confront and collide with those that are taken for granted, some interlock and reform to produce new combinations and fresh conceptual structures. Since Galileo recharted the heavens to imbed them within the same physical universe as the earth, he may be depicted as one of the founders of modern consciousness. The skies are no longer seen as belonging to a higher reality but as part of the human world and as governable by the generalizations that people make. The possibility of transforming the pedagogic frameworks of theories of teachers may be increased not only by their similar willingness to explore and to look for the new, but also by their readiness to be awakened to the ongoing creation of different worlds of consciousness. Schooling and teacher education may need to be reconstrued as revolving not around the authority of politicians and educational researchers but around that of teachers and their students.

What we know as teachers is grounded both in our personal assumptions and in those that are socially shared. As a result, the classroom world of teaching and learning that we seek to understand always remains just on the horizons of our thoughts. In this book, ways of launching out from what are our admittedly limited perspectives are suggested in order to enable us to transcend present certainties and dogmatisms. How we might go about looking for what might turn out, and even help bring it about, is proposed. This, then, is a book about differences and similarities in teachers' perspectives, in their viewpoints or constructs, and about some ways forward to their constant transformation. If the course of their understandings (and mine!) appears to be complex, overlapping and chaotic, fragmentary and inconsistent, it may also prove to be interesting and even entertaining. The knowledge of tomorrow may be based on the fairy tale of today.

Various theoretical and practical constructs are drawn on first to generate some exploratory hypotheses and, then, in a tighter move, to develop a more coherent system of explanatory principles to better guide and safeguard education. In the first chapters, a case study approach is used to indicate the significance of recent trends towards centralized control of the curriculum and teacher education. A counter 'cosmology' or interpretive position is then proposed in which teacher education is reviewed and reconceptualized as involving nothing less than the critical retheorizing of teaching or the continuing transformation of perspectives. The account of their making and unmaking draws upon the work of such scholars as Vygotsky, Kelly, Britton, Bruner and Habermas.

The treatment of actual teachers' perspectives and their gradual or sudden reorientation is first computational and then narrative in emphasis. These bipolar alternatives characterize Kelly's (1955, 1969) psychology of personal constructs and provide the theoretical basis of my book. The approach in the later chapters initially may seem more traditional, analytic and quantitative, as the Repertory grid methodology is used to study teaching both by statistically mapping teachers' major constellations of ideas and by questioning their centrally informing structures. The second approach is clearly more qualitative and literary as various storytelling procedures and methods of analysis and of response are explored. Both sets of approaches encourage teachers to create their own new coherences and to remodel their perspectives.

While the temptation still remains either to rush to pursue 'the' plot or to decide whether or not a teaching life represents a comedy or tragedy, any version of teaching, like life itself, is not a series of symmetrically arranged and easily subsumed experiences. Any understanding of teaching is a net that we weave and throw, reweave and rethrow, as we seek incorrigibly to make teaching our own. Seeking to classify any perspective is both a risk and a threat to our individual uniqueness. As William James cautioned, probably even a crab would be filled with outrage if it could hear us dismissing it, without apology, as simply a crustacean. Instead it would insist: 'I am no such thing. I am MYSELF, MYSELF alone!' (cited by Nolte, 1966, p. 166).

Pat Diamond

Acknowledgements

Adopting the Kellyian position that journal articles and book chapters ought like a theory be good for something, some of my previous work is represented here in a rearranged and edited form, together with new material, to constitute a book of its own. By being reconsidered, reconstrued and retitled, they now hopefully cohere into a single volume rather than remaining just a collection of papers. Any greater coherence is largely due to the efforts and encouragement of the series editor, Christopher Day.

I am grateful to the following for their kind permission to include versions of material of my own that first appeared elsewhere:

Academic Press Limited, London, for 'Becoming a teacher: An altering eye'. In D. Bannister (ed.), *Issues and Approaches in Personal Construct Theory*, 1985, pp. 15–35.

Australian Association for the Teaching of English, Sydney, for 'You always end up with conflict: An account of constraints in teaching'. In R. D. Eagleson (ed.), *English in the Eighties*, 1982, pp. 31–43.

Australian Educational Researcher for 'Benchmarks for progress or teacher education on the rails', 1988, **15**, 1–7.

Australian Journal of Education for 'Fixed role treatment: Enacting alternative scenarios', 1985, **29**, 161–73.

International Journal of Personal Construct Psychology (Hemisphere Publishing Corporation) for 'An essential perspective: Reconstructing and reconstruing teachers' stories', 1990, **3**, 63–76.

Journal of Education for Teaching for 'Teachers can change: A Kellyian interpretation', 1982, **8**, 163–73.

Oxford University Press, Melbourne, for 'How to succeed in composition:

Large as life, and twice as natural'. In R. Arnold (ed.), *Timely Voices*, 1983, pp. 96–110.

Psychology in the Schools (Clinical Publishing Company) for 'The use of fixed role treatment in teaching', 1983, **20**, 74–82.

Routledge & Kegan Paul, London, for 'Turning on teachers' own constructs'. In F. Fransella and L. F. Thomas (eds.), *Experimenting with Personal Construct Theory*, 1988, pp. 175–84.

I am also grateful to the following for their permission to reproduce original material:

Academic Press Limited, London, for quotations from Kelly, G. A. (1970), 'A brief introduction to personal construct theory'. In D. Bannister (ed.), *Perspectives in Personal Construct Theory*, pp. 1–29.

Academic Press Limited, London, for quotations from Kelly, G. A. (1977), 'The psychology of the unknown'. In D. Bannister (ed.), *New Perspectives in Personal Construct Theory*, pp. 1–19.

John Wiley & Sons Inc., New York, for quotations from B. Maher (ed.), *Clinical Psychology and Personality* (1969).

W. W. Norton, New York, for quotations from Kelly, G. A. and Routledge (1955), *The Psychology of Personal Constructs*, Vols 1 and 2.

Teaching: a besieged perspective

A collision of metaphors

Johnson (1988) described the 1980s as the age of 'control chic', of reborn puritanism that seeks satisfaction in acts of control. As the French etymology of *control* shows, the fundamental procedure consists of the act of checking 'against' (*contre*) a 'list' (*rolle*). Teachers in such an age need to read or interpret events as a boundless text that structures their culture and controls their world view so extensively that 'the hell they are in remains invisible to them' (Johnson, 1988, p. 313). They need to learn to reread and to recast both in opposition to, and then beyond, both the best selling and official pronouncements of educational doom. By becoming stronger readers and more self-aware writers, teachers can learn to read the imprisoning text of official discourse for its contradictions and then deliberately incorporate it into personally richer and more self-conscious, alternative perspectives (see Chapter 7). Sight can yield to insight, and knowledge can be restructured in empowering programmes of teacher education. Teachers need to release themselves from the paralysis of being hurried and harried.

The period of rationalization in education has been quickly followed by one of outright assault. While the conceptualization of curriculum and teacher education always seemed previously to be pushed into the background by the more immediate problems of reorganization and student numbers, governments have now seized the political and moral initiative from their academic critics to force a technocratic reconceptualization based on the simplisms of productivity and accountability. What is needed by way of defence is a counter-design at a deeper and more significant level of theorizing about the nature of schooling and teacher education and about the kinds of intellectual and executive attributes they require. Rather than dwelling on the logistical implications of contraction and centralist intervention, there is an opportunity to concentrate on conceptual and qualitative issues and to provide an analysis and rationale for teacher education in terms of its own unique character.

The improvement in standards in education is increasingly being viewed as a mechanistic process: the teachers must be subject experts capable of matching their teaching to particular age phases and then be held accountable for the success of their students' learning. The too familiar call is for 'benchmarks' for progress. A developmental perspective is used in this chapter first to capture something of the accumulating significances of the moves in North America, England and Australia towards centralized control of the curriculum. Next, a basis is provided for the growth of a critical response from teacher education to counter these increasing levels of government control.

North America

Countering attacks on all sides, teachers could be forgiven for a crisis of confidence. Jacoby (1987) alleged both that the West faced collapse since the universities had been swamped with intellectual laziness and that their obsession with openness and equality had produced a generation bereft of civilization. Hirsch (1987) similarly accused schools of serving their students poorly and of failing to teach Western culture. He blamed their cultural relativism and progressivism for occasioning an educational Fall. To aid in bringing about an educational Redemption, he drew up a list of 5000 items, alphabetized from 'abbreviation' to 'Zurich', as a dictionary of cultural literacy to establish guideposts for teachers and students. Hirsch advised that core knowledge ought to be put into school textbooks so that progress in piling up specific information could be measured. His four 'mono' items included *monogamy*, *mononucleosis*, *monopoly* and *monotheism*, and perhaps ironically could be taken as setting the conservative agenda for education. The list was understandably criticized as a traditionalist *Trivial Pursuit* that was over-demanding, culturally selective and pedagogically regressive. Its misuse was predicted to be not a danger but a certainty. For Scholes (1988, p. 331), Hirsch's proposal was not just a little off target but was 'voodoo education offering a quick cheap fix for massive educational problems, while ignoring the intractable realities that underlie those problems'. Hirsch was seen as calmly, if unconsciously, distorting his sources and as failing to draw the proper conclusions from his own examples. 'It is because the sweetly reasonable facade of his book is just that – a facade – that *Cultural Literacy* is such a bizarre and dangerous book' (p. 332).

Bloom (1988) also sensationally claimed that teachers have failed both to teach and to educate. When interviewed, he not only lamented 'the impoverishment of the souls of today's students', but also 'teachers who don't know anything' (*The Times*, 15 February 1988). For Bloom, declines in reading skills and corresponding jumps in illiteracy had led to calls for a national core curriculum. He described higher education as having all the resources but none of the intellectual vision. The decline in Britain was conceded not to be as serious as that in North America because of a 'continuing love affair with Shakespeare'. While Bloom's educational jeremiad and those of the above concluded that the only hope for the West was in a rebirth of real inquiry, it is disturbing that they require teachers to know everything well except themselves and their professional practice. Knowing classrooms is not a second-rate activity for those who cannot grasp the broader issues. Knowledge is not something to be consumed but is to be made and remade.

England

The Times (16 February 1988) published a list of 100 questions that its panel of experts thought sixth-form school leavers should be able to answer. As an example of this *Mastermind* or quiz approach to education, question 66 asked ambiguously and even derivatively: 'The words *monotonous*, *monogram* and *monochrome* have the same first four letters. What do they [*sic*] mean?'

In answer to another question, 61 of the sample of 97 students were able to identify Kenneth Baker as the then Secretary of State for Education. Three days later, *The Times* asked yet another panel of its experts to compile a list of 50 books that every child aged 3–7, 8–11 and 12–18 years should read. Baker had earlier encouraged the use of age-related texts in order to test reading. His Education Reform Act (ERA) may be even greater historical significance than the Butler Act of 1944, as it marks a shift to the central control of education. The Act has been also characterized as regressive and instrumental in purpose (see Simon and Whitbread, 1988). The focus is shifted from the developing child, from education as a liberating experience, to a production model.

Baker was reported in 'Straight to the Core' as gladly subscribing to Bloom's view that there is a core of knowledge that all educated citizens should possess and which schools had a duty to impart. 'We must have a national curriculum. . . . I sense a yearning among teachers for a more explicit framework' (*The Times*, 18 February 1988). He added that it was for the professional educators and researchers to defend what they had done: 'The gurus are in the dock! Let them work out why they have failed so dismally.' There was not enough rigour, not demanding enough teaching. The basic skills had to be taught first! Being decent in the Victorian sense of the word should infuse everything that went on in the school. He confirmed that 'thankfully Shakespeare was alive and well up and down the land' (*The Times*, 28 February 1988). The conservative reformers at least realize that language represents the key issue.

Baker (1988) compiled a verse book of English history that itself was reviewed as 'History verse and verse'. He had misspelt Boudicca, the subject of his first selection, and then in his explanatory note confused the places and dates relating to Julius Caesar. Still, a week later, Baker confessed that English was very close to his heart. The headline of 'Grammar under sentence of death' ominously gave way to that of 'Back to Grammar'. Kingman, the chairman of the report on the *Teaching of the English Language* (1988), was given a copy of Baker's pre-emptive media statement just 10 minutes before his own scheduled press conference. The committee itself had previously been widely acknowledged as hand picked by the government and even denounced as 'rigged' (Rosen, 1988, p. 3). It had been confidently expected that it would reject the Bullock Report (1975) and even avenge those findings.

Though the Kingman Report described teachers as not confident in their own explicit knowledge and though it agreed that there were both inadequacies in the professional education of teachers and a misunderstanding of the nature of children learning, Baker still found that the report was not prescriptive enough. Accordingly, he rebuffed his own committee by announcing that grammar lessons would return. It is essential, he announced, that attainment targets provide specific enough objectives for pupils, teachers, parents and others to have a clear idea of what is expected (*The Times*, 30 April 1988).

The Department of Science (DES) report, *The New Teacher in School* (HMI, 1982), had earlier reported as disturbing the finding of Her Majesty's Inspectorate of Schools (HMI) that, in many of the aspects of initial training, at least a fifth of the teachers felt ill-prepared. In a similar spirit of dire disclosure, 28 higher education institutions in England were placed on a blacklist published by the Economic and Social Research Council. Too few of their postgraduate students had submitted funded doctorates on time and a sanctions policy debarred them from further funding. *The Times Higher Education Supplement* reported that 'postgraduates are giving poor value' (19 February 1988). A poll reported two days later described universities as fearing for their independence and six out of ten academics as considering giving up their jobs. The real income of universities had fallen by a third in the decade.

The new conservatives not only felt that 'language meant business', but also believed that business could teach education a thing or two. In 1913, Bobbit had called for scientific management techniques to be applied to the more 'backward' institution of education because 'education is a shaping process as much as the manufacture of steel rails' (p. 11). More recently, Angela Rumbold, the then British Minister of State at the Department of Education who was responsible for teacher training, argued that courses should be linked to industry and commerce. In addition, as *The Times* (11 May 1988) reported, she hoped that middle-aged executives, 'tired of the rat-race and tempted by the prospect of a less stressful career', might be able to 'bypass the usual training requirements' to become teachers under plans being considered. The Thatcherite ministers believed that teaching required an infusion of new blood if schools were to meet the challenge of the national curriculum of 11 compulsory subjects. And it was at hand. Middle-aged executives, their mortgages paid and their children off their hands, might accept a drop in salary for a less stressful job.

Australia

In Australia, a similar sequence of events was enacted. John Dawkins, the former Minister for Trade, took up a combined portfolio for Employment, Education and Training. In December 1987, he circulated a policy discussion document that called for an examination of the performance of higher education and the effective discharge of its roles, especially in relation to the economic strength and vitality of the nation. The limited conceptual vocabulary was familiar and invoked: 'economic and labour market considerations, economies of scale, cost-effective delivery, effectiveness and efficiency, market demand, funding options, incentives for change' and 'adequate levels of accountability'.

The development of internationally competitive manufacturing and service industries required a more highly skilled and better educated workforce. Economic considerations pointed to the need for an appropriate mix of graduates. Traditional generalist courses might need to be supplemented by shorter career-oriented courses. The sharp decline in teacher education and humanities enrolments might continue, together with the correspondingly strong growth in business studies or economics. A high priority was to be accorded to the enhancement of mathematics and science and a review of teacher education in these discipline areas was begun. The market ideology also underpinned Dawkins' white paper so that the success of institutions in addressing the issue of completion rates would become increasingly important in the context of 'a resource allocation process that will focus increasingly on assessment of overall institutional performance' (Dawkins, 1988a, p. 17).

Institutions were to compete for resources on the basis of merit and capacity. Those that chose to be part of the unified system of higher education would benefit from liberalized resourcing arrangements and a share in the growth in the system. The funding system would respond to institutional performance and the achievement of agreed goals. While there was token admission that the development of reliable performance indicators is a difficult issue, particularly for service industries such as education whose activities are 'not always readily assessable in terms of their quantity, quality, durability and reliability' (Dawkins, 1988a, p. 41), the clear definition of roles and responsibilities was nevertheless held to be the prerequisite to effective management. Staffing issues would relate to quality, productivity and adaptability. What was clear was that, while greater flexibility and autonomy for higher education were not on the immediate agenda, greater government control was.

In May 1988, Dawkins released a paper on strengthening Australia's schools. The familiar solution was to call for the development of a common curriculum framework that set out 'the major areas of knowledge and the most appropriate mix of skills and experience for students in all the years of schooling' (Dawkins, 1988b, p. 4). There was a need for higher general levels of literacy, numeracy and analytical skills and a major feature of the new framework should be criteria for assessing the achievement of objectives. There needed to be a common national approach to 'benchmarks for measuring student achievement. Assessing school performance ... must be a further objective of a national effort.'

Because the quality of teaching was central to the quality of schools, the means of improving the initial and ongoing training of teachers needed to be examined. National guidelines for the registration of teachers might be needed. A National Board for Employment, Education and Training would help maximize the nation's investment in education and guarantee a return.

Teacher education: a counteroffensive

In the *Time* essay of 5 February 1990, it was alleged that, while students 'feel exceedingly good about doing bad', there is an urgent need for 'real achievement and real learning'. Such headlines, crisis journalism, reports and government expressions so influence public perceptions that teacher education is seen to be in trouble. And it is. But only from the widespread, technocratic challenge to higher education and to teachers to prove themselves. The general strategy, at least in Britain, is one of blaming the victim, 'bringing the teaching profession to heel, intimidating dissident voices, and closing down options' (Rosen, 1988, p. 4). There is mounting pressure for education to justify its existence within an entrepreneurial culture and largely in terms of its relevance to the needs of industry and commerce. The great debate has become the great divide, with the field containing a good deal of prejudice and unfounded assertion.

The DES report on *The New Teacher in School* (HMI, 1982) recommended a 'more effective process of quality control' (p. 81) of teacher graduates. As in the white paper *Teacher Quality* (1983), the HMI seemed to adopt its political patrons' technological view of improvement in education. In the DES report, *Quality in Schools: The Initial Training of Teachers* (1987), the HMI recommended forcefully that the future response of teacher training institutions to the new demands made by teaching and government policies 'should be radical' (p. 21). This would involve many in a reappraisal of entire courses. What was needed could not be achieved by addition and minor modification. A great deal remained to be done and there was little point in continued tinkering. Teacher education programmes had to be 'revamped from top to bottom'.

The burden of accountability, however, is to be borne at the bottom, because the principles of scientific management and technocratic efficiency emphasize hierarchically structured, 'top-down' models of accountability. Those at the bottom are held accountable by those at the top – power resides with the accountants and not with the teachers. Administrators and politicians seek to use an 'objective' knowledge base about teacher competencies in order to hold teachers and their educators directly accountable. The reign of generic managers and practical experts, together with management by objectives of human material, seeks to empower some few by depriving many. This represents a resurgence of dogmatic authority in government and in education. Scientific management and hierarchical accountability tend to distort and even destroy dialogue. Critical exchange and collaboration yield to orders and conformity. As the crisis in teacher education is 'talked up', teachers are 'talked down'.

The development of teachers' counterperspectives or the reconstruction of meaning may consist less of a monotonously relentless march along a bench surface or worktop towards an ultimate, government-decreed, cost-effective and monopolistic reality than an endless scaling of yet more peaks. What was thought to be the pinnacle or the higher ground turns out to be just one more look-out for a glimpse of still more removed and less accessible vistas. Each solution eventually dissolves to become part of yet another problem. In Chapter 2, four peaks of the teacher education terrain are discerned and mapped, beginning with competency-based approaches, progressing through personalistic approaches and culminating in language and learning and meaning-based approaches. Rather than merely attaining 'adequate levels of accountability', teacher education involves the continual transformation of perspective. However, while the narrow path to politicians' 'fixed purpose is laid with iron rails, wherein [their] souls are grooved to run' (Melville, 1851, p. 172), the engines of unswerving economic rationalism will whir on and any dream of an ascent to a higher reality must struggle to resist mere adjustment to the expedient.

2

Conceptualizations of teacher education

Traditional models of primary and secondary teacher education systems leading to a teaching certificate are very similar throughout the world. The basic structure includes three components: academic preparation in the subjects or disciplines that the student is to teach; theoretical foundations of professional education, such as courses in the philosophy, history, sociology and psychology of education; and the student practicum or teaching in some form of internship. However, at a more fundamental level, each form of teacher education is based on a characteristic ideology or set of guiding assumptions.

Four major movements in teacher education may be identified and described in terms of a bipolar distinction between academic-competency and progressive-personalistic approaches. An inquiry-oriented synthesis is offered in this chapter that is based on a theory of language and learning (Vygotsky, 1962; Britton, 1970) combined with a theory of personal constructs (Kelly, 1955). While recognizing the uniqueness of individuals, learning is acknowledged as deeply social, and the goal of pre- and in-service teacher education is seen as no less than the transformation or the critical retheorizing both of teachers' perspectives and of teacher education.

Competency-based teacher education (CBTE)

According to Joyce and Clift (1984), no field could better use the magical properties of the Phoenix in order to be reborn from a desperate situation than teacher education. It is surrounded by vigorous critics. By way of response, Joyce and Clift advocated a competency or performance-based approach to pre-service teacher education that segmented the acts of effective teachers and then applied systems approaches so that the effective teachers were used as models to train beginning teachers. They stressed the need for an academic knowledge base and characterized present teaching as 'a theoryless, totally pragmatic frame of reference' (Joyce and Clift, 1984, p. 8). Beginning teachers should be trained by university scholars who are themselves concerned primarily with what takes place in classrooms and who are also skilled teachers. A united sequence of experiences should be promoted that gradually inducts beginning professionals by teaching some of the early skills of teaching.

The DES report (HMI, 1982, p. 25) on the training of teachers had adopted a similar skills-based approach and asked why, when there was then no shortage of applicants for teaching posts, should as many as 'a quarter of the teachers in the sample be markedly deficient in a number of the teaching skills which they might have been expected to acquire through their training?' The skills that HMI had assessed at high levels of inference related to the quality of: teacher–pupil relationships and class management; planning and preparation of work; match of work to pupils; teaching process; language used in the classroom; and questioning techniques. However, as McNamara (1984) concluded, while it is sensible to presume that there are a few, but only a few, skills that a beginning teacher must be able to demonstrate, such as being able to write clearly on the blackboard and to project the voice to the back of the classroom, once beginning teachers move beyond these to questioning or motivational skills, 'there are no established procedures' (p. 294) that they must adopt in order to teach effectively.

The recurring trend to accountability has its origins in the public disenchantment with teacher education as expressed in the earlier criticisms of the 1960s. CBTE centred on the prior specification of competencies that teachers should acquire in order to perform certain tasks. These competencies were to be determined at various points in their preparation in relation to three general areas: their knowledge, teaching behaviour and pupils' payoff-knowledge. However, CBTE has been opposed both because of its limited philosophical base and because of its limited knowledge base. Continued research on such sterile behaviouristic definitions of teaching seems unlikely to provide an adequate basis for training teachers.

Popkewitz et al. (1979) proposed that much of the difficulty in attempting such behaviouristic approaches to teacher education comes from the underlying empirical-analytic model of most educational research. Such an approach sees the purpose of inquiry as the discovery of a deductive system of propositions or scientific laws, which are then to be used to predict and control teaching and learning. These human activities are assumed to have characteristics that exist independently of the intentions of the classroom actors. According to Heath and Neilson (1974), the research agenda is limited to a few concerns such as seeking to influence beginning teachers' performance through micro-teaching or the use of the Flanders' interaction analysis programme. Both approaches specify desirable teaching behaviours, seek to teach them and then to measure the effects.

A related 'scientistic' concern of much in-service teacher education is to identify empirical links between teaching behaviours and increments in student outcomes. Research is to identify these competencies and to enshrine the laws governing such pedagogical acts. However, such process–product or research and development approaches are unable to come to grips with the fundamental intentionality or distinctive viewpoints of teachers. Popkewitz *et al.* (1979) found that, despite the hundreds of presage–process–product studies, there have been almost none of the actual processes of teacher education as they unfold over time. No theory has developed from the accumulation of all the discrete behaviouristic data and even the precise list of important competencies does not exist. Mastering and pursuing the craft of teaching goes far beyond repetitions and routines.

The resurgence of interest in CBTE and its government endorsement has flowed from recent attempts to apply to teacher education the limited concep-tualizations of skills training derived from industrial and military settings. In a familiar scenario, the repertoire of behaviours to be mastered was to be analysed to specify less complex components, which were then taught by direct instruction and practice with corrective feedback. However, from a human developmentalist perspective, teachers are acknowledged as uniquely inten-tional persons rather than as merely programmable objects. CBTE clearly does not serve teachers and their epistemologies. Teachers are deprived of power precisely by putting the production and distribution of knowledge about teaching into the hands of politicians and researchers who set the criteria of teacher competence and performance. Teachers' personal knowledge and purposes are ignored and they are held accountable to those of others.

The delineation of specific behavioural objectives, prior to or early in a teacher-learning sequence, assumes that the teacher as learner is inert and passive, that there is a stable body of knowledge and of skills and that there are fixed approaches to learning. However, from an alternative constructivist position, the teacher is seen as essentially active and world-making. The goal of teacher education may be nothing less than the creation of perspectives and of worlds.

Personalistic teacher education (PTE)

PTE approaches differ sharply from the competency-based position that teachers should be taught a set repertoire of classroom strategies, which they then learn to apply. PTE argues instead that teachers each develop in a unique way and that to be educated they must be helped to formulate adequate selves, personal agendas and keen appreciations of the needs of others. The under-lying metaphor of PTE is one of organic growth rather than of mechanistic

functioning. Its epistemological foundations are broadly phenomenological
and rely heavily on perceptual and developmental psychology. In addition,
there is a pervasive historical tradition that emphasizes the teacher's indi-
vidualism. Thus, HMI (1982) found that the personal qualities of teachers were
often the decisive factor in their effectiveness, and in the DES white paper
(HMI, 1987) they agreed that teacher personality is as important as specific
knowledge and skills.

Combs (1972) adopted such a humanist perspective and outlined effective
teacher education as a highly personalized affair, one which is dependent on
the prospective teachers' development of appropriate systems of beliefs
leading to greater psychological maturity. Educating effective teachers involves
promoting their 'becoming' or their personal discovery rather than training
them precisely in how to teach. Teacher education should emphasize meanings rather than imitated behaviours and should focus more on the teachers'
subjective experiences and less on objectively gathered or received information about teaching and learning. In addition, becoming an effective teacher
requires secure and accepting conditions. Individual agency both enables and
is reliant on social communion.

Joyce (1975) described PTE as focusing on the uniqueness and dignity of the
individual to produce what he described as an idiosyncratic conception of
teaching and learning. Because this approach accentuates empathetic and
caring relationships between equals rather than any standardization of teacher
competencies and learner outcomes, some critics may also describe one of its
possible dangers as that of producing eccentricity. However, PTE seeks to
supply an inquiry-orientation involving a developmental approach where the
programme provides for a balance between action and reflection as it attempts
to foster selfhood and human growth.

There is general agreement that a personal growth model of pre- and
in-service teacher education is now needed and that it might well contain a
view of the existential person who hopes to become and remain a teacher. In
such an approach, the teacher internalizes a combination of courses and
attempts to sort out the pedagogical role or teacher self considered appropriate from many possible selves (see Chapter 3). While personal development
has remained the missing link in teacher education, it may be supplied by a
theory such as Kelly's (1955) psychology of personal constructs, which focuses
on individual change and understanding.

Dewey (1938) also claimed that an emotionally engaging experience must
be followed by reflective analysis if qualitative changes in growth and development are to occur. Because knowledge is perceived as emergent and ever-
changing, the teacher's essential task is to learn how to create knowledge and
not merely to receive it. Such a knowing or reformist view of teacher education
is learner-centred, problem-oriented and hypothesis-generating. The challenge is so to personalize the mechanisms of teacher education as to take
account of the human beings in them. Through the mediation of supportive

teacher educators, they can be made aware of the significance of their learning activities and by internalization come to perform cognitive functions that were originally experienced in collaboration with their teachers (see Chapters 4 and 5).

Language and learning in teacher education (LLTE)

Like the humanistic growth model, the development of language and learning has remained at best an accompanying and subsidiary goal in teacher education. In *Learning to Teach: Teaching to Learn*, Dow (1979) described a case study of an experimental course at the University of Melbourne. Much of her book drew from the students' diaries written as they went through the course. Dow postulated that for each student the problem of becoming a teacher was an intensely personal and individual matter. Each of them needed as much experience as possible in thinking and acting autonomously in their year of professional preparation. After 15 years of working in the programme, Dow (1979) concluded that students, in learning to teach, can learn to learn; indeed, they are forced to be more self-conscious and less self-centred about their own learning.

In Chapter 4 of the Bullock Report, Britton (1975, p. 47) argued that 'it is the role that language plays in *generating* knowledge and *producing new forms* of behaviour that typifies human existence'. Accordingly, teachers can be seen as characteristically symbolizing, representing to themselves the people and events that make up teaching for them. They create an inner representation of the world of teaching as they encounter it. The accumulated representation provides them with a past and a future and all their actions are influenced by and performed within their body of expectations. They interpret what they perceive at any given moment by relating it to their past experiences and then respond to it in the light of that interpretation. Language is the crucially significant way in which they shape their experience and represent the world to themselves. It is the prime means by which generalized representations can be constructed. As Britton (1975, p. 48) summed up the role of language in learning, we have to generalize from particular representations of past experiences in order to apply them to new ones, and 'language helps us to do this by providing a ready means of classifying [our] experiences'.

However, language provides more than a thesaurus or an inventory of words. Not only does it organize teachers' experience of teaching, but also their continued intellectual growth is dependent on its providing them with vital predicting equipment. When they confront problematic situations, as in beginning to teach or after having taught for a very long time, language can form their statements of possibilities and then can be used to elaborate further these hypotheses. The effort to formulate an hypothesis results in a 'spelling out' to which they may return in the light of further experiences and in search of other possibilities. A continuing sense of pedagogy is able to be brought up to date by each teacher.

At the various North American sites of the National Writing Project, teacher educators seized on the opportunities for reflection and inquiry that a language and learning or a psycho-rhetorical approach affords in relation to the tacit knowledge of practitioners (see Emig, 1983). This provided the basis of teacher-driven in-service teacher education. Later chapters offer a number of written ways in which teachers' knowledge of their own pedagogy can be documented and appreciated. Kellyian methodology supplies a plan of action for the invasion of the little known and a control for the risks that are entailed.

In LLTE, spoken or written formulations become a source from which, by a kind of continual spiral, further questions and fresh hypotheses may be posed and drawn. As Britton argued, the statement that we have made becomes an object of our own contemplation and a spur to further thinking. The higher thought processes become possible to the person who in this way 'learns to turn his [or her] linguistic activities back upon his [or her] own formulations' (Britton, 1975, p. 49). Rather than just communicating nuggets of information, language helps teachers to generate knowledge and to make worlds of understanding for themselves. To bring knowledge or texts into being is a formulating process accomplished by means of language, whether in speech, writing or thought. These supply the verbal aspects of construing experience and of turning experienced events into meanings.

Mastery of language, and especially writing, is fundamental to the achievement of abstract and reflective thinking. The constancy of writing added to the immediacy of speech enables teachers to reflect upon their meanings and to acquire a new level of control, a critical awareness of their own thought processes. Writing makes an essential contribution to the development of teachers' pedagogical theories, including their sense of their own teaching selves, as once they write what they mean they can see if they still mean it. As Kelly (1969, p. 56) wrote in the autobiography of his theory:

> Not only ... [do] the words man uses give and hold the structure of his thought, but, more particularly, the names by which he calls himself give and hold the structure of his personality. Each of us invests [himself] with a particular kind of meaning.

To write is to become empowered in profoundly, uniquely human ways. People can change as a consequence of their redefinitions of themselves and teachers can explore different versions of their pedagogical selves. Writing is the symbolic process of creating worlds through texts, and, if these text worlds prove unsatisfactory, of recreating them through revision. These text worlds can be easily and readily shared with self.

These texts can also be shared with others. Teacher education or growth of mind is not merely to be thought of as a lonely voyage of each on his or her own. Human consciousness is achieved by the internalization of shared social behaviour – and this is Vygotsky's central contention (see Britton, 1987). The source of learning is not just discovery and invention but also negotiation and sharing. Learning is not only the generation of personally significant meanings but it is also the process by which teachers may grow into the intellectual life of those around them. Education is an effect of self in community.

As Kelly (1955) insisted, learning is not just a special class of psychological processes but is synonymous with any and all such processes. Learning is what makes a teacher a person. It derives its special status from the recurring processes by which individuals make sense of their worlds rather than by passively receiving and reproducing the wisdom of others. Learning takes place, however, through social interaction. The very essence of such develop-ment lies 'in the collision of mature cultural forms of behaviour with the primitive (i.e. natural) forms that characterize the [young person's] behaviour' (Vygotsky, 1981, p. 151).

All genuine learning involves discovery, but this is not to suppose that the learner is left to his or her own devices. This convergence of forces from two lines of development, natural and social, leads to development so that the former products are transformed by contact with the latter. For Bruner (1986, p. 25), human learning has been too often depicted in the paradigm of a lone organizer pitted against nature – 'whether in the model of the behaviourist's organism shaping up responses to fit the geometrics and probabilities of the world of stimuli', or in the personalistic model where learners struggle single-handed to strike some equilibrium between the world to themselves or themselves to the world. In contrast, learning by transaction and transforma-tion makes it possible for teachers to proceed Phoenix-like beyond their present perspective or level of development to achieve higher ground and new consciousness (see Chapter 5).

Perspective transformation in teacher education (PTTE)

Part of the problem of making sense of consciousness is the problem of finding an appropriate metaphor. Jaynes (1979) indicated that the most common metaphors used to indicate our awareness of the nature and properties of consciousness are drawn from our experience of vision and three-dimensional space. The most usual group of words used to characterize mental events are visual. Thus we 'see' solutions to problems, the best of which may be 'brilliant', while others may be 'obscure'. The person may be 'brighter, watchful, Argus-eyed' and 'clear-headed' as opposed to 'dull' and 'fuzzy minded'! The mind-space to which these words apply is a metaphor of actual space in which we can 'approach' a problem from some 'viewpoint' or 'perspective', 'grapple' with its difficulties and 'comprehend' the parts of the problem (Jaynes, 1979, pp. 55–6). Each individual forms a microcosm of the known world and, as a private universe, it has its own processes of growth and decay, whether slow or sudden. Each metaphored mind-space has its own separate centre, its 'starer' or mind's eye.

Kelly's (1959, p. 12) theory of interpretive frameworks is founded on the belief that 'each man creates his own way of seeing the world in which he lives; the world does not create them for him'. If events are subject to as great a variety of interpretations as we have wits to devise, even the most obvious occurrences of daily life in the classroom 'might appear utterly transformed if we are inventive enough to construe them differently' (Kelly, 1970, p. 1).

According to Wildemeersch and Leirman (1988), a meaning perspective can be considered as a reservoir of interpretation patterns that are individually generated and collectively transmitted as, for example, in pre- and in-service teacher education. This stock of knowledge, definitions, aspirations and actions is composed of basic assumptions that function as an implicit or tacit horizon, the limits of which are difficult to transcend. As a framework, however, it supports and integrates the actions of people in a meaningful whole. It is only when its familiar interpretation patterns fail that new explanations of old experiences are then searched for. The provision of alternative viewpoints, differing interpretations and criticism are essential to the encounter and may be provided by narrative experience, sharing and dialogue.

Mezirow et al. (1975) drew upon the interactionist concepts of Becker et al. (1961) to adopt the organizing construct of perspective. Mezirow (1978, 1981) described extension of the existential horizon as transformation of perspective, which he then defined as an epistemic change. This involves an emancipatory process of critical awareness that reconstitutes the ways in which we see ourselves and our relationships to permit a new integration of experience and action. If a meaning perspective is an orienting framework or personal paradigm (Merizow, 1989), its transformation consists in a restructuring of the person's own action-orienting self-understanding.

To reconcile the emphasis on the individual with a comprehensive theory of social change, Merizow (1981) used the social philosophy of Habermas (1971) to present a theory of education that posited three generic forms of knowledge or learning domains: the technical, the social and the emancipatory. These areas correspond to three learning goals: for academic knowledge and task-related competence; for interpersonal understanding and communication; and for perspective or meaning transformation. While the empirical-analytic model assists in the understanding of the skills relating to CBTE, the second goal of communication requires an LLTE approach, as it focuses on helping teachers interpret the ways that they and others know and construct meanings and also interact. The historical-hermeneutic sciences are appropriate in the second domain.

Perspective transformation, the process cental to the third area, is a cognitive form of PTE and involves helping beginning and experienced teachers to gain access both to their own and alternative meaning perspectives from which to interpret reality. The second and third areas serve two functions, the interpersonal and the representational, which are centrally important to teacher education as they incorporate the knower into the process of knowledge production. Vygotsky (1962) believed that language has these two functions, communicative and cognitive. The former property links it to its roots in social action and the latter to its uniquely encoding powers, which enable self-reflexivity.

Communication and generalization are linked, as the world of experience must be greatly simplified and generalized before it can be translated into symbols. The 'experiencing of experiences' (Vygotsky, 1979, p. 19) depends upon the self-reflexive application of the representational function of language to its own representational properties. While language used for the interpersonal aspects of communicative interactions produces inner speech, language used to represent the referential aspects of language produces logic and abstract thought. Later stages of development represent new levels in the organization and restructuring of consciousness.

The essential role that meaning making plays in the ways that individuals constitute their existence is an axiom of existential, phenomenological, Gestalt, Piagetian, perception theorist and Kellyian-construct approaches. Perspective transformation consists in the reorganization or confirmation of cognitive structures in the light of experience. As a shift in world view, 'governing gaze' (Emig, 1983, p. 160) or preferred way of perceiving reality, it involves the active, engaged and personal making and unmaking of a set of hypotheses so that a 'web of meaning' or personal construct system is elaborated or extended. Into every act of such fundamental expansion or re-cognizing of understanding 'there enters a passionate contribution of the person knowing what is being known. This coefficient is no mere imperfection but a vital component of his [or her] knowledge' (Polanyi, 1958, p. viii).

If learning by transformation or by the remodelling of consciousness represents the highest level of teacher development, it must yield to teachers a fuller and richer understanding of teaching which enhances their abilities to deal with personal and professional difficulties. In turn, their sphere of personal agency is widened and they can begin to confront social problems and injustices. Underlying this approach to teacher education is the metaphor of reinvention, liberation or freeing of consciousness. The teacher with transformed perspective is free from a lack of skills and abilities, free from unsupportable attitudes and free from the unwarranted control of unjustified beliefs. If CBTE ignores questions of individual purpose, as well as those of substance and value, perspective transformation approaches seek to focus upon them. The aim is understanding beyond knowledge, which is achieved through the continual reaching out to fresh versions of teaching and learning.

The means to perspective transformation is critical self-awareness of, and emancipatory insight into, the reasons for present difficulties. As Mezirow (1981, p. 5) wrote, 'the knowledge of self-reflection includ[es] interest in the way one's history and biography has expressed itself in the way one sees onself, one's roles and social expectations'. Self-knowledge yields critical consciousness of how teachers' meaning perspective both reflects and distorts, prisms and imprisons their own versions of reality and of what factors sustain the consciousness it represents. The process of perspective transformation alters an initially non-reflective consciousness by emancipatory action. Because it increases a critical sense of agency over self and one's life, it represents the most significant of the three kinds of learning posited by Habermas. Action can become more self-directed and consciously controlled. By reflecting on their own constructs and practices, teachers can enlarge first their awareness and then their capacity to direct it more fruitfully. Thomas (1979) appropriately expanded Kelly's theory with a self-awareness corollary; that is, to the extent that a person construes his or her own constructions of experience, he or she acquires consciousness. To the extent that person construes his or her own processes of construction, he or she acquires more complete awareness of themselves as a person. More complete awareness is the means of perspective transformation.

Although the most distinctively adult domain of learning, the epistemological empowerment of teachers to engage in knowledge production is the least known paradigm in adult education. In a rare exception, Mezirow (1981) reported extensive interviews of women re-entering college, which showed their movement through the existential challenges of new learning. This involved the negotiation of an irregular succession of transformations in meaning perspective and the continued consideration of 'the structure of psycho-cultural assumptions within which new experience is assimilated and transformed by one's past experience' (Mezirow, 1981, p. 6).

Perspective transformation is the emancipatory process of becoming critically aware of how these structures or schemata both enable and constrain the way teachers see themselves and their relationships and then reconstituting this structure to permit a more discriminating integration of experience and acting upon these new understandings. Teachers need not be confined by their own personal history. It may be that only through preparedness to take a personal stance towards, or stake in, teaching, that they can have the right to teach. As Salmon (1988) wrote, to teach should mean to offer what is personally meaningful. And teaching comes to have personal meaning only if one has reflected deeply on one's own journey so far through life. That entails struggling to see how one's own experience is encompassed by what one understands. 'You are yourself, in some sense, what you teach' (Salmon, 1988, p. 37).

This process of awareness involves seeking to be alert to the extent to which what seems meaningful to teachers reflects a very particular standpoint. As Kelly (1955) hypothesized, only then can teachers move towards new perspectives that are more inclusive, discriminating and integrating of experience. The aim of pre- and in-service teacher education is greater order, interrelatedness and complexity. Through this quest for meaning, a vantage point is gained from which to view teaching in a broader perspective. Teacher self is then better able to understand and better anticipate events.

To the extent that teachers can change their constructs, they can free themselves from domination by limited constructs and open up new possibilities or perspectives for the solution of problems. The process of revising constructs in the light of experience defines such learning. The teacher whose previous convictions encompass a broad perspective, and which are cast in terms of principles rather than rules, has a much better chance of discovering those alternatives, which may lead eventually to his or her emancipation. Teacher education construed as perspective transformation involves teachers in reconstrual, in revising their intellectual structures and attaining a new balance. The fundamental objective of this book is to urge a change in the perception and evaluation of the familiar data of the classroom and to encourage teachers to find revolutionary new ways of teaching.

3

Pre-service teacher education: expansion of perspective

Nias (1989) found almost no information about who and what teachers perceive themselves to be. Few attempts have been made to present detailed portrayals of the reality of teaching from the standpoint of teachers themselves. If the emphasis in the first two chapters has been on broad conceptualizations of teaching, the emphasis in the next three chapters is on the actual teaching of live teachers in their own classrooms, that is, on the perspectival development and practice of beginning and experienced teachers.

As argued in Chapter 2, perspective redefinition or transformation is a cognitive form of personalistic teacher education that employs language and learning techniques to help teachers in their struggle to shift their perspectives. They first focus and then gain and express ever wider worlds of teaching. These techniques include symbolic interactionist, Kellyian and autobiographical or literary procedures. Just as perception implies the active participation of the knower, all teachers must inevitably acknowledge that they see the world of the classroom from a centre lying within themselves.

In devising school-based programmes of pre-service education, teacher educators need to resist the temptation to aim at short-term goals such as mastery of the survival skills relating to discipline. They need to seek instead to help beginning teachers to use practice teaching to become students of their own teaching. Long-term understanding of education rather than short-term mastery of practical classroom problems is the goal. The focus needs to be on educational ideas and principles that illustrate the realities of teaching. Unless prospective teachers have their taken-for-granted experience of teaching, as well as its current models, challenged by the provision of ideals and alternative standards of effective practice, they may be susceptible to excessive realism and too readily accept the existing kinds of teaching that they observe as rigidly setting the limits of the possible.

Field studies confirm that student teaching may contribute to the adoption of a utilitarian perspective that conflicts with the expressed purposes of programmes of teacher preparation. According to Feiman-Nemser (1983), this research questions the validity of the widespread belief that practical school experience necessarily produces good teachers. The student teachers who remain content with mastery of skills may continue to define the most significant problem of teaching as discipline and to respond by keeping their students busy and doing things – but may not necessarily help them to learn for themselves.

Thoughtful support may make it possible to learn in pre-service training the kind of practice that then leads to many years of continuing to learn to teach. Beginning teachers need to be helped to cultivate and to have sustained their capacity to learn from their teaching and to grow in their work. However, with few exceptions, the existing research reveals very little about the actual conduct of teacher preparation and in-service training. Very little is said about on-the-job learning to teach and its 'dailyness'. However, it is impossible to understand and to improve the impact of teacher education without knowing still more about what it is like.

Studies of pre-service perspectives

Apart from some case studies of student teachers, Calderhead (1988a) noted that very little is yet known about the interpretive frameworks or personal construct systems with which they approach their experiencing of learning to teach. Knowles (1987) believed that teacher biographies or teacher role-related life-histories are important in understanding beginning teacher think-ing and professional socialization. His exploratory case study traced two female graduate pre-service teachers, one of whom failed the teaching practice and one who succeeded. Data were collected by using a variety of ethnographic approaches: journals, classroom observations, interviews, student reflection papers and life-history accounts. Journal writing was found to encourage their reflective thinking. Such recognition of the contribution of personal perspect-ives has only recently been addressed.

Tardif (1985) also used a combination of data-gathering techniques to follow four student teachers throughout three semesters to highlight how they defined themselves in the process of becoming teachers. Using an approach based on symbolic interactionism, she found that there were similarities and commonalities in the ways the student teachers reacted to the practicum. A set of prevailing perspectives towards teaching seemed to evolve in which the two major themes related to feeling like a teacher and adopting classroom teaching behaviour. Transformation was also identified as a form of higher-level development but was not discussed in any detail.

Calderhead (1988a) followed a group of 10 student teachers through their course in order to study their emerging understandings. Interview transcripts revealed that the first 2 weeks of teaching practice was a highly stressful period because of the feeling of being constantly watched and assessed. Much of their own teaching was deliberately modelled on that of their cooperating or supervising teachers in order to fit in with existing routines. They acquired the characteristics as required by the situations in which they participated and as exhibited by the professionals they encountered most directly.

They seemed to learn much in the early part of the course, especially about classroom management, but this quickly reached a plateau midway through. Anxiety was replaced by exhaustion and daily teaching became almost like a treadmill. Learning to teach became perceived as a kind of recurring driving test in which there was a series of skills they had to perform and on which they would be assessed again and again. The aim was to pass and perhaps afterwards they could teach as they wanted. The students also displayed a series of teaching actions to please their university tutors and to gain credit in their particular assessment. They discounted, however, much of the tutors' observations.

During the second half of the course, most students reported feeling more relaxed with children. They remained unsure, however, of the kinds of criteria they ought to use when evaluating their own teaching. Their analysis of teaching still seemed fairly superficial. Calderhead (1988a) concluded that research has still obtained little conceptual grasp of the actual reflective processes involved in professional learning and that further research is needed to identify such concerns in more detail.

One team of researchers (Ryan et al., 1979) sought to describe the life-space of a first-year teacher and focused on 18 new teachers' perceptions of their beginning careers. They were interviewed and observed and two fairly self-evident themes emerged: the inevitability of limitations of any teacher preparation programme, and the value of first-hand or practice teaching experiences.

Becoming a teacher: an altering eye

Bruner (1987, p. 32) concluded that his life as a student of mind has taught him the one incontrovertible lesson, that is, that mind is never free of precommitment: indeed, there is 'no innocent eye'. There are instead only hypotheses, versions and expected scenarios. Teaching, like life, is a story and, however incoherently assembled, it is better understood by considering other possible ways in which it can be told. As for William Blake (1805), 'the eye altering alters all'.

Dewey (1950) described the altering process of scientific inquiry as resembling the most refined form of reflective thinking. Five general features of this experience include: initial confusion or doubt, as one is implicated in an incomplete situation whose full character is not yet determined; a conjectural anticipation or tentative hypothesis; a careful exploration and analysis; a consequent elaboration and refinement of the hypothesis; and taking one's stand upon the projected hypothesis as a plan of action and testing it. Every projected hypothesis is a plan of action. However, this is not to deny the uniqueness of individuals, because 'methods remain the personal concern, approach, and attack of an individual, and no catalogue can ever exhaust their diversity of form and tint' (Dewey, 1950, p. 173).

Kelly personally acknowledged, if seldom attributed, his own debt to Dewey and Vygotsky. Theirs is a common insistence on the way that people interact with their world and actively process rather than passively store their experiences. People are seen as developing sets of hypotheses or construct systems in which their present abstractions are tentatively placed on past experiences and then later are projected upon future events in order to cope with those events. These hypotheses are individually constructed from experience and through them each person sees and interprets the world. The system is more like a pair of spectacles than a filing cabinet or knapsack, because not only does the person get information through it but it even conditions what and how he or she experiences. The construct system busily seeks verification and does not wait.

If people can understand their own perspectives, as well as those of others, they can not only understand their past but they can also make predictions about their likely behaviour in a given situation, such as the classroom, because they know something about what that series of events is likely to mean to themselves and others. Kelly invented the Repertory grid to help people exhibit their construct systems. If grids are elicited over a salient period of time and then reflected upon, the processes of change, growth and decline in each person's perspective may be interpreted variously as expansion or contraction, massive or negligible, ordered or chaotic, sudden or gradual, desirable or not. The aim of Diamond's (1985a) study was to encourage teachers during their year of professional preparation first to see into and then out of themselves.

Like other professionals in training, student teachers come to grips with the specific domain of teaching expertise by plotting their observations (or elements) against their dimensions of appraisal (or constructs) and by testing their constructs against their observations. Because the Repertory grid expresses the finite systems of cross-references between the personal observations that are made and the personal constructs that are devised, it acts as a kind of psychological equivalent of a rough ground plane mirror of their developing conceptual networks. As Thomas (1976, p. 3) wrote, the direct experience of discovering emerging patterns of personal meanings within oneself, by oneself, or in close conversation with another, enables an individual 'to set out on a voyage of exploration, within the private space of his or her own phenomenal world. No one returns from such a voyage unchanged.' FOCUS-ed grids (see below) are one major step towards making this process of change available.

Seventeen students who were reading for the postgraduate diploma in education (DipEd) at the University of Queensland with a core of educational studies and a variety of curriculum subjects as offered in secondary schools were helped to study their own development of perspective. They completed Repertory grids at the beginning, midway through and at the end of the year-long course; that is, after teaching once in primary and twice in secondary schools.

I explained that the purpose of the study was to explore the student teachers' views of teaching and of people over the course of the academic year. The first step was to identify the elements or items extending over the range of convenience – in this instance, the people to be compared. A common set of 16 elements (see Table 1) was derived from studies by Adams-Webber and Mirc (1976) and by Pope (1978). Roles 4, 5 and 6 together represent part of the active, creative process at the heart of the experience of being a teacher self. They help us distinguish between positive will (bringing about what one has accepted from others as appropriate for a teacher), counter-will (opposing the demands inappropriately made on one as a teacher) and creative will (bringing about what one wants as an autonomous teacher). As Rank (1936) suggested, these aspects may unfold in the course of development.

The grids were elicited by offering the student teachers a randomly derived list of triads and asking how two of the three elements were alike in some important way that distinguished them from the third. The students were asked

Table 1   Role title list (pre-service)

Figure number	Figure description
1	Self
2	Past self
3	Ideal self
4	Teacher I am
5	Teacher I fear to be
6	Teacher I would like to be
7	Mother
8	Father
9	Siblings
10	Spouse/steady
11	Friends
12	Pupils
13	Principal and deputy
14	Subject master
15	Supervising teacher
16	University tutor

to write a word or short phrase description under 'construct' indicating similarity and the opposite of the characteristics under 'contrast'. Each element was finally rated on the scales defined by the pairs of poles from 1 to 5 (that is, from most to least on each of the emergent poles) and their allotted values were recorded. This process continued for about 90 minutes, using different triads, until 12 constructs were identified.

On each of the three occasions, only the original elements were preserved, so that comparative analyses of change between successive grids could be made. Because one of the usually avowed aims of teacher education is the development of fresh and even radically different perspectives, this provided opportunity for any new constructs to emerge. Care was taken to ensure that the statistical calculations did not distract the students from the focusing procedure and the major purpose of the study; that is, the revelation and exploration of personal and shared patterns of meaning as they evolved over the year. To further promote feelings of ownership and self-invention, the teachers were encouraged to keep a learning log or teaching journal. Devising a fable or dialogue was one of the activities suggested to aid the process of making personal sense out of the course experiences. Emig (1983) also advocated frequent and inescapable opportunities for composing, especially reflexively.

The FOCUS computer program (Thomas, 1979; Shaw, 1980) was used to analyse each teacher's three grids. This programme provided a two-way cluster analysis in each case in order to re-order the rows of constructs and the columns of elements so as to produce a FOCUS-ed grid in which there was the least variation between adjacent constructs and adjacent elements. This analysis was done with respect to the way the elements were ordered by the constructs. The relationships were visualized as tree diagrams for the constructs and the elements that showed the highest similarities in the clusters.

The SOCIOGRIDS program (Thomas, 1979; Shaw, 1980) helped on the same three occasions to explore the similarity and differences in construing between the teachers. This technique is based on Kelly's commonality assumption that there are areas of shared meaning among individuals. The programme analysed each set of Repertory grids elicited from the group and based similarity in terms of the ordering of the element set. Three mode grids were thus extracted from the group, and in each case the number of modal constructs was comparable to the number of constructs in the separate individual grids. Thomas *et al.* (1976) originally suggested considering every occasion where two constructs from different grids are adjacent and weighting the occurrence with the level of match in which it occurs. Using this stable but sensitive measure, each of the mode grids was made up of those constructs that clustered adjacently at a high level of match. The constructs chosen as representatives of group construing were firmly based in the ways in which the elements had been construed similarly by the majority of the group.

SOCIOGRIDS also produced three sequences of sociometric diagrams

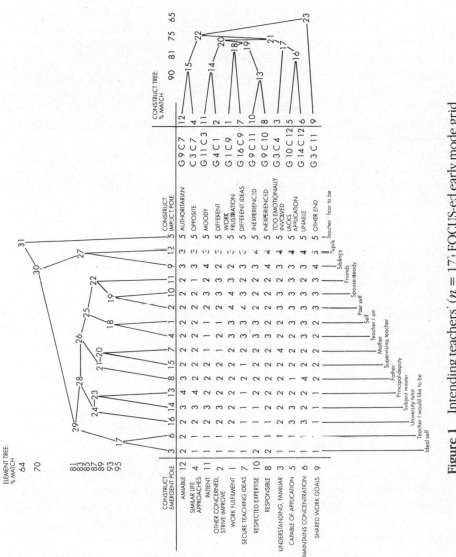

Figure 1 Intending teachers' ($n = 17$) FOCUS-ed early mode grid

designated *socionets* from the matrix of similarity measures between pairs of individual student teachers' grids. The highest related pair on each occasion was featured as a subgroup where commonality of construing occurred, followed by the subgroups defined by the rank ordering of all the similar measures. As the pattern of links or nets developed, both modal and more isolated construers were located. The former have often been described as star construers. While the socionets revealed the structural properties of the group, the actual content of the shared construing was exhibited in each of the mode grids. These in turn were seen as being representative of group perspectives (see Becker *et al.*, 1961).

As Fig. 1 shows, at the beginning of the diploma course, after the primary and before the first secondary practice, the 17 intending teachers formed one superordinate construct at the 75 percent level. In terms of their verbal labels, this large cluster or superordinate idea seemed to express an overarching concern for professional and personal qualities. One very wide element set was formed tightly at the 80 percent level, together with *siblings* and *pupils* paired at the 83 percent level. The *teacher I am* was delineated as very patient, amiable, similar in life approaches, concerned about others and striving to improve, understanding and familiar, and capable of application and sharing work goals. The group was undecided about themselves on 5 of their 12 construct dimensions. Pupils were similarly not as yet clearly perceived on six scales but, in contrast, they were seen negatively on the remaining ones; that is, as very inexperienced, too emotionally involved, lacking application, unable to concentrate, and not at all sharing teachers' work goals. While the 68 percent level of match between the *teacher I am* and *pupils* seems to indicate a degree of initial goodwill, the acceptance may have been conditional.

After the first secondary practicum midway through the course, the group formed two superordinates marginally more tightly at the 78 percent level (see Fig. 2). The wider cluster grouped constructs quite categorically and, in addition to some tightness in formation, the construct labels suggest greater emphasis on pupils and a movement towards more instrumental concerns relating to motivation, discipline and managerial effectiveness.

A more inclusive element set was formed, leaving only the *teach I fear to be* in isolation. However, *pupils* was one of the last elements to be related to the other significant people. It was associated at an even lower level than previously with the *teach I am* (64 percent) and delineated clearly but negatively on seven dimensions as very immature, childlike, followers, not having teachers' goals, dependent, not confident, and not future-oriented. A more pre-emptive view of *pupils* seemed to be emerging. The *teacher I am*, in contrast, was seen more decisively and positively as mature in knowledge, caring, emotionally strong, adult and friendly.

At the conclusion of the course, the intending teachers construed people and teaching somewhat abstractly in terms of two equally broad and more closely knit superordinate ideas. Despite a literal concern for clients, the elements

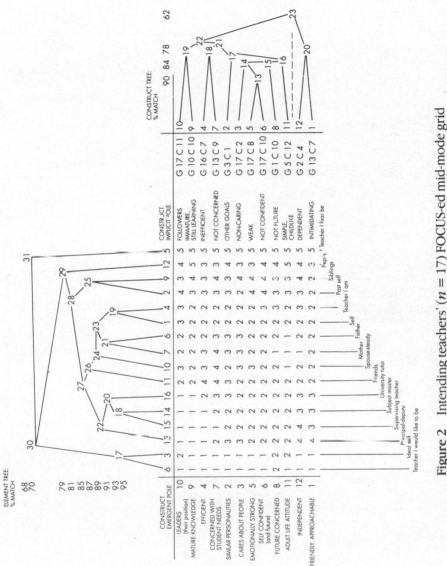

Figure 2 Intending teachers' (*n* = 17) FOCUS-ed mid-mode grid

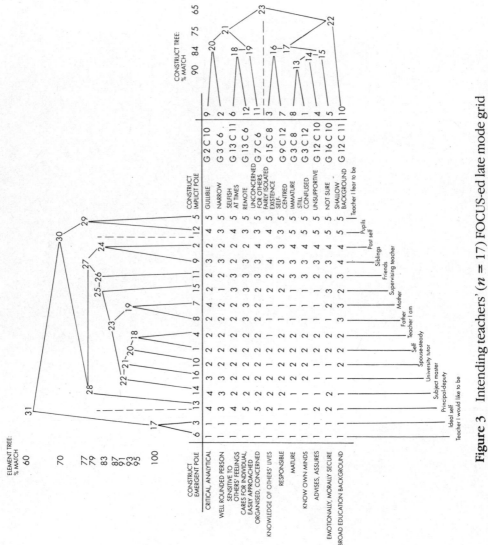

Figure 3 Intending teachers' (*n* = 17) FOCUS-ed late mode grid

Table 2 Meaningfulness index (the amount of undecided responses)[a]

Grid	Element	
	Teacher I am	*Pupils*
Early	5	6
Middle	4	5
Late	0	3
Total	9	14

[a]($n = 12$ on each occasion.)

were split into three exclusive groups. The largest cluster consisted of *self*, *the teacher I am*, *spouse*, *university tutor*, *subject master*, *past self*, *siblings*, *friends* and *supervising teacher*. The second group paired *ideal self* and the *teacher I would like to be* at the 100 percent level, while the third was made up of *pupils* and the *teacher I fear to be* (77 percent). The intending teachers' element boundaries were firmly defined by personal and pedagogic ideals on the one hand, and by pupils and the undesirable teacher on the other (Fig. 3).

The teachers were now sure on nine dimensions how *pupils* should be described; that is, they were extremely immature, confused, unsupportive, unsure emotionally and morally, and with a very shallow educational background. In contrast, the *teacher I am* was definitely and positively seen on all 12 dimensions. As shown in Table 2, fewer undecided responses (ratings of 3) were made to the *teacher I am* and *pupils* in the mode grid as the year progressed. These two key elements were increasingly perceived in more meaningful but opposed ways.

In order to analyse the changing relationship between the pedagogical self and the client elements, the degrees of association between the *teacher I am* and *self*, the *teacher I would like to be*, the *teacher I fear to be* and *pupils* are shown during the early, middle and late components of the course in Table 3. These matching scores are drawn from the matrix of element matching scores for each of the 17 teachers and from the group as a whole. This provided a sensitive indication of the degree to which their perspectives were redefined.

The group began with a very high degree of role identification that was maintained and even intensified (95 percent) over the year. Teaching is very inclusive as teacher 4 (Anne) also found:

> I have wanted to be a teacher for as long as I can remember and by the end of the second prac. I knew it was still the right decision. . . . Though it's hard, I really love working with kids.

While the group as a whole initially experienced only a moderate degree of compatibility (64 percent) between the teachers they were and the teachers

Table 3 Percentage of association with *teacher I am* during the three components of the course*

Teacher number	Early				Middle				Late			
	Self	Teacher I would like to be	Teacher I fear to be	Pupils	Self	Teacher I would like to be	Teacher I fear to be	Pupils	Self	Teacher I would like to be	Teacher I fear to be	Pupils
Mode	93	64	35	68	93	68	33	64	95	79	20	43
1	83	56	52	68	85	81	41	70	95	85	35	70
2	79	64	45	64	68	56	62	66	81	50	62	81
3	93	81	25	62	93	81	25	62	91	87	16	37
4	87	75	31	75	86	72	26	60	95	85	14	52
6	89	77	33	45	81	68	43	41	72	79	20	25
7	85	77	25	64	91	70	43	70	89	89	16	52
8	93	68	29	68	79	58	68	70	87	60	50	79
9	83	66	39	37	56	87	12	25	79	66	39	52
10	87	56	62	66	87	66	55	73	91	68	45	75
11	62	56	54	68	77	59	48	65	79	72	37	72
12	87	77	37	72	87	81	27	70	83	64	39	60
13	91	58	45	66	85	47	54	58	83	85	12	50
14	81	62	41	62	87	68	33	75	87	75	29	72
15	77	56	60	50	76	60	55	60	60	39	75	64
16	87	77	27	54	81	75	31	58	79	83	20	54
17	93	85	14	68	93	81	20	70	83	75	25	54
18	95	72	64	72	97	64	45	85	91	68	45	75

* Note: Teacher 5 left the course

they wanted to be, this level of congruence steadily increased to reach almost 80 percent. Their process of accommodating reality and ideal was dramatized by teacher 18 (Sonya) in a short dialogue between two facets of her teaching self, the *teacher I am* (TA) and the *teacher I would like to be* (TB):

TA: When I'm teaching I always think about you and how I don't measure up to you and worst of all that I never will.

TB: Look, it's not a problem. Think of me as something you can work towards. Just don't let it get you down. Your trouble is that you want to achieve as quickly as possible. Instead you should let time work on you. Experience is the best teacher you know.

The teachers also continued to escape from the *teacher I fear to be*. However, the gap that opened up between them and pupils threatened to yawn into an abyss by the end of the year with 43 percent replacing the previously closer levels of match. Not surprisingly, pupils proved to be a major construing problem for these intending teachers.

The socionets revealed how closely on each of the three occasions each teacher's perceptions of the similarities and differences between the elements resembled each other teacher's. The summary in Table 4 shows that teachers 3 (Paula) and 10 (Helen) were consistently most like the group in their construing, while teacher 9 (Sam) was most unlike in his. These three construers were selected on this basis and studied in detail so that the broad changes in perspectives might be related to more particular personal influences.

Members of the Centre for the Study of Human Learning at Brunel University (see Thomas, 1979) have stressed that caution must be exercised when conclusions are drawn from grid studies. While the grid remains a useful technique for accessing psychological processes that are not easily perceived, and while it helps to focus individual perceptions, premature attempts to generalize towards collective meanings are hazardous. However, as shown in Table 3, a mode grid can provide a common referent with which each individual can compare his or her grid. Grids serve as a conversational heuristic for the development of perspectives.

Teacher 3: Paula

Paula was preparing to teach English and social science. As a star construer, she associated her *self* with the *teacher I would like to be*, the *teacher I fear to be* and

Table 4   Kinds of construers

Grid	Modal	Isolated
Early	3, 10, 16, 17	9, 15, 13
Middle	1, 3, 10, 14, 18	2, 4, 7, 9, 16
Late	3, 6, 7, 10, 13	1, 4, 9, 12

pupils almost exactly as the group did during the year (see Table 3). Paula wrote in one of her last journal entries, 'Mostly what I want is to be successful at teaching – to be sure of myself and confident in what I do as a teacher.' Fuller (1969) also found that most beginning teachers really want to succeed, and they highly relate personal and pedagogical elements.

Like most of the group, Paula reported some final estrangement from *pupils*. Her degree of association with them first remained at 62 percent but then ebbed dramatically to 37 percent by the end of the year. Though she was practising at a difficult government school, she wrote:

> I don't fear them so much as feel uncertain about them. The aspect of having to control and discipline pupils is one of the major causes of my ambiguity of feeling towards them. Lack of experience in handling discipline promotes feelings of uncertainty about one's ability to cope.

Paula felt similar uncertainty and hostility towards her own younger *siblings*.

Aesops's Fable of 'The Man and the Ass' summed up the experience of becoming a teacher for Paula:

> No-one can please everyone all the time. . . . Truly, it is very confusing and frustrating to find that when you please either superiors, teachers, parents, pupils or yourself more often than not you displease someone else. . . . We are like the donkey, pushed and pulled from one side to the other. It is difficult to fulfil successfully the dual role of University student and intending teacher.

Teacher 10: Helen

Helen intended teaching English as a second language and social science. She felt that the content of her superordinate constructs changed greatly: inexperience and lack of confidence were finally replaced by being questioning, analytical and critical. Helen's increased confidence was reflected in her teaching self moving progressively closer to her ideal and to her pupils, but away from her feared teacher component. Unlike the group as a whole, Helen's degree of empathy with pupils increased from 66 through 73 to 75 percent. She wrote: 'I've got to adore my kids this semester. They're lovely!' Helen attributed this 'altering eye' to a change in her practising schools. She ended the year in a small, fee-paying girls' school where she was supported and encouraged and thus able to relax and be innovative in her teaching. Helen represented her own delayed self-recognition by drawing upon T. S. Eliot's 'Four Quartets' (1944) and at the end of all her exploration knew 'the place for the first time' (p. 43).

Teacher 9: Sam

Sam had enrolled to teach chemistry and general science but the Army Reserve was his main declared interest. Sam's association of *self* and *teacher* dropped from 83 to 56 percent by mid-year. Though this score improved to 79 percent, his level of commitment seemed well below that of the group (95 percent). Sam also began being more alienated from *pupils*, though this gap also lessened.

Sam wrote that his previous and continuing role as an instructor in the Reserve stood him in better stead than the diploma as a form of teacher preparation. Early in the year he explained:

> I'm disappointed in the course. I expected to be taught definite ways of teaching. . . . I fear my commitments to the Reserve are going to suffer. I'd better read only what is necessary and no more.

Midway through the year, Sam found that it was easy to 'get by':

> During prac. even preparation the night before is not really required. I find myself looking forward to my Army courses. The Army takes me away from the Uni. environment where I feel enclosed, chained to the ivory tower. Hopefully I'll last it out to the end. My mind has been totally oriented towards the army.

During the last practice session, Sam admitted with typical candour: 'I'm not even as interested as I was last time. I don't think I have been as receptive through the course as I should have been.' Perhaps Jarrell's (1964) sleeping bats objectify Sam's reluctant induction into teaching as it was presented in the course. When the adventurous little brown bat asked them to keep their eyes open for a while during the day, they refused even to try, saying 'we just don't want to' (p. 4).

Teacher 14: Carole

As a representative or star construer in the middle of the year, Carole is included as one of the 'little brown bats' by way of contrast. Carole was practising to teach English and social science and felt that her growing commitment to her pupils (62, 75 and 72 percent) resulted from '*self* butting in on the *teacher I am* and establishing a more humane relationship with them'. If she did not get to know the students as individuals, she felt she would be just an actor performing in front of a blank class.

Carole's construct matching scores show an interesting progression in her teaching perspective. In her first grid the greatest match was between flexibility, imagination, trying new things and being energetic. In the second, it was between strives to achieve, shy/quiet, bored with repetition and zest for life. In the third, it was between cares for children and sensitive to others' feelings. Carole was increasingly focusing on pupils and her responses to them.

Çarole's personal approach to teaching was evidenced by the way in which she construed the *pupils* over the year. In the first grid, she described them in positive terms (imaginative, innovative, in constant change, fairly energetic, flexible). In the second grid, she was also optimistic (zest for life, feeling out new ground, bored with repetition, needing specific knowledge), but her view was tempered by some of the realities that had been discovered in the first practicum period. Her perspective in the third grid remained enthusiastic (casual, sense of humour, confident) with the exception of describing them as fairly selfish. Despite this criticism, her grids showed an increasingly higher match between the *teacher I am* and *students* (62, 75 and 72 percent) than did those of the mode grids (68, 64 and 43 percent).

It is interesting to note that, while *teacher I am* and *pupils* were associated comparatively highly, *self* and *pupils* gained an even higher percentage match of 77, 66 and 81 percent, for the three grids, respectively. This establishes an important distinction for Carole between *self* and the *teacher I am*. Perhaps this conflict can be explained in terms both of her wanting to establish close and supportive relationships with pupils and of her need also to adopt a distant, authoritarian position in the classroom (see Coulter, 1987). Carole wrote:

> Since I am not by nature an authoritative [*sic*] person, I felt a greater rapport with students as *self*. I often felt the presence of this conflict while I was on prac., and found it difficult at times to reconcile dealing with the pupils on a personal basis, yet still maintaining my authority.

Sam was tougher minded and typically ready to declare his position. He wrote: 'You just have to let the kids know who's boss. You can't be their friend. That's all.'

In the main, the intending teachers found the practice periods extremely threatening. As Sonya commented: 'It's eight weeks of living in a pressure cooker!' Teacher 15 felt besieged by a headmaster described as 'Mr. Law', by name as well as deed. The style of a beginning teacher's haircut was of crucial importance in that school. Teacher 16 experienced conflict with an authority figure closer to home, her father, who had refused to allow her to apply for a government scholarship, alleging she should not become a teacher because 'she didn't even know that cows could swim'. Hirsch (1987) might have also shared his reservations!

The socialization of these 17 beginning professionals into their occupational roles was able to be indexed at least in part by their developing a common frame of reference or perspective. Their homogeneity in outlook was revealed in the three successive mode or group grids that were extracted. Also, the socionets showed there were subgroups that differed not only in their subject specialization but also in their perception and acceptance of *pupils*. In general, however, there were increasing levels of role identification and of reconciliation with teaching ideals. Finally, there was a marked shift in meaningful 'seeing' as more definite rather than undecided responses were made to the centrally important elements of the *teacher I am* and *pupils*.

The mode constructs or group perspective changed from expressing personal and professional qualities to categorical, instrumental concerns that then merged either with discipline- or pupil-centred ideas. Another feature of the transformation of perspective was the tendency for the large construct clusters also to become progressively tighter over the year (75, 78 and 84 percent) in their degree of association. While Adams-Webber and Mirc (1976) reported increased levels of integration in student teachers' viewpoints after practice teaching, this present pattern might mean that the teachers' construct systems were becoming increasingly less permeable; that is, rather than broadening their perspective and construing teaching in different ways, they were seeing it in a tight, rigid way, from an increasingly fixed point of view. However, the same pattern could indicate instead that the group became more firm or confident in their construing. As constructs gradually take shape, they are then more tightly formulated and prepared for an eventual rigorous test for either confirmation or disconfirmation. It seems that neither tight nor loose construing is an end in itself and that instead development of perspective consists of multistage movement between the two.

Uncertainty about initial teaching ideas was reduced by real-life classroom experience. Carole, for example, explained she had first imagined the worst and had to grope desperately for more secure ideas. In her fable, another beginning teacher (teacher 11) described the shifts from recent graduate to student teacher and finally to qualified teacher:

> In DipEd, as in any fairy tale, just when you think you're out of the woods, there is suddenly more to them than you ever imagined. Just when you think you have escaped to an open quiet place it turns out you're still in them. Even later the woods you're wandering in turn out to be yourself.

According to Carole, the group's construct matching scores revealed a progression in content from respected expertise/responsibility as an important construct in the first grid to emotionally strong and self-confident in the second grid. This could indicate a change from the idealistic pre-practice climate to that of the post-practice where many of the student teachers found that their ideals had to be abandoned in order to maintain order and to please their supervising teachers. The constructs of the third grid, mature, knows own mind, advises, assures and emotionally, morally secure, perhaps indicate that the student teachers were coming to confront the discipline problem and were looking to their own maturity and were taking on an advisory rather than a dictatorial role.

What is clear is that the group had adopted a narrow, pessimistic perspective on *pupils* at the end of the year. This empathetic gap is discussed by Fuller (1969), who found it less characteristic of more experienced teachers who focus on gaining satisfaction from pupils rather than on controlling them. The group's negative, apprehensive view of *pupils* may have been conditioned by the need to control them. This restriction is revealed in how they characterized *pupils* as lacking in background, application and concentration, and as being immature, childlike and unsupportive. Many of the beginning teachers expressed a fear of losing control, of not being able 'to get on top' in the classroom. Veenman (1984) and Tardif (1985) described this shift to more traditional authoritarian and custodial views as commonly found. Becoming a teacher in these circumstances can be a growth-inhibiting experience.

When the star and the more isolated perspectives were studied in detail, only Anne with a very few others was found to have finished the year by positively construing *pupils*. Yet even her development was highly personal, as it represented something of a 'comeback'. Anne agreed that her most interesting figures related to *pupils* (see Table 3):

> In the first prac. I saw 75 percent similarity between *pupils* and the *teacher I am*, while in second prac. there was a dramatic 30 percent drop to 45 percent. I was quite apprehensive towards students at first; however, there were no discipline problems at primary prac. As a result I didn't feel threatened by them – nor I would imagine them by me. I hardly felt like a teacher at all, just like a large version of a student pretending to be a teacher. I therefore saw the students as allies, more so than the teachers. This accounts for the 75 percent match.
>
> In the second prac. at high school (in the first weeks especially) frustration best describes my reaction to students. I didn't feel I could communicate with them at all and being in an all boys' school didn't help. Although I enjoyed planning lessons, I often felt so nervous I didn't think I could give them. I felt extremely threatened and intimidated by students, more so out of the classroom than in it. By the end of the prac. I felt more relaxed and began to take more to the role of teacher than student. However, this anxiety about students accounts for the drop in similarity to 45 percent.
>
> The figure for third prac. shows a change again from the former prac. session. Students have levelled out to a 52 percent match with the *teacher I am*. My explanation for this is that I now have a clearer idea of how I view students, whereas I didn't before. In the previous two pracs. my opinion of them went from one extreme to the other. In the third prac. I enjoyed interaction with students and I felt they liked me. This feeling of acceptance played a big part in the return of my relaxation and confidence. I left third prac. feeling enthusiastic about further teaching and clearly identifying with my role as a teacher.

Anne became much more self-assured and less threatened. During her earlier secondary practicum she had written:

> I'm terrified I'm going to make a fool of myself. I don't quite know what to make of the students. They just stare at me. Like the little boy sitting in

front of me today when I was marking some work. He turned round and looked at me all the while as if I were the most fascinating thing he had ever seen. I decided to ignore him.

Bannister (1981) commented on this kind of limbo state that, although qualifying as teachers, many students feel they are still psychologically students just playing the role of teacher. Teacher 1 (Mitzi) also experienced this kind of initial dissociation of herself from her teacher self:

First high school lesson: Me playing a double role. One is the make believe teacher at the front and me going beyond myself to where I was the other watching the person out front, giggling and gazing in disbelief: 'That surely can't be you out there!' How do you become a 'real' teacher and not just an authority figure?

The only opportunity for a full transition from playing to becoming a teacher would be in the two remaining practical periods. For some students it may not occur until their induction year of full-time teaching.

Mitzi changed from being a typical or modal construer in the middle of the year to an isolate. She wrote: '*Pupils* remained with me as *teacher* at the same 70 percent, so much higher than the mode. I interpret this as me being more perceptive of and responsive to the needs of students.' In contrast, teacher 6 (Peter) was salient in being consistently dissociated from *pupils* over the year (see Table 3). Peter explained his beliefs:

Most of the teachers I felt were successful during my school days were those who had a good deal of distance but respect from their pupils. I chose to follow this 'formula for success'. Those teachers who tried to be less formal and more familiar were generally abused and 'stirred' to the maximum. I don't mind being high on a kid's 'Death List'. It's actually a mark of respect.

Sam left the course convinced of the fact that corporal punishment was essential. He insisted that school discipline would collapse without the occasional 'belting' with the cane. Unlike Carole, Anne and Mitzi, both Peter and Sam were training to teach science and seemed to reflect only two of the concerns of beginning teachers as found by Fuller (1969); that is, they focused on 'my performance' and 'discipline' but not on being 'pupil-centred'. While it may be easier to look into self than to see how self is looked out of, the subject or curriculum specialization of the first degree may also affect these kinds of capacities.

During training, the group's teacher self moved increasingly farther away from its feared, negative counterpart (35, 33 and 20 percent). In contrast, Mitzi reported a very high match (52 percent) between these elements after the first practicum:

I found myself doing things which seemed too unnatural and out of character for me. My supervising teacher was often quite severe with some students for what seemed really trivial matters. Yet I felt obliged at times (through lack of experience I guess) to imitate her when faced with the unknown – but I felt bad about it.

A higher than group match was noted by Grant (teacher 8) during his second practice period. He too was tempted to deny his own *self*:

I swung like a pendulum. My thoughts, attitudes and feelings reacted violently to reality. I changed quickly to my supervising teacher's form. I did not like it but it was successful in dealing with the volatile situation of school. Anyway he would be assessing me. I still don't like the shift away from myself though.

This perspectival difficulty remained unresolved at the end of the year for Paula:

I felt conflict about being liked by the students and at the same time being a disciplinarian. This concern about being able to handle discipline and control situations is at the forefront of my worries. Most teachers seem to feel control is the real test of a teacher.

Though Paula felt almost coerced, Peter's metaphor of 'The Sorcerer's Apprentice' contains elements of his willing collaboration and portrays transformation of perspective as the putting on of another kind of thinking cap:

I am the greenhorn apprentice and the wizards are my supervising teachers. They demonstrate to me the 'magic' of transforming uncooperative students into willing learners. Maybe the kids are even cleverer and allow the teachers to give them what they need for the exams.

Headmaster and *deputy*, apart from *pupils*, were most consistently and closely linked to the *teacher I fear to be*. For Mitzi, administrators were 'so far removed from the real life situation of classes that they only present negative images of teaching. For me they are rigid, out of touch with youth, egocentric and judge people, especially students, too hard.' Most of the group, however, described their administrators as knowledgeable of others, very responsible and mature. They were seen as knowing their own minds and being sure of their advice to others.

What in teacher preparation, apart from further professional experience, might make a difference and close even these gaps needs to be studied. Loosening activities or licensing student teachers to loosen their constructs of people and teaching might be required. Such procedures include role playing what it feels like to be a pupil in school or teaching each other and then reversing roles. By participating even in fantasy in the perspectives of pupils and in glimpsing their world, teachers may come to grasp more readily their future clients' points of view (see Chapter 5). Such experiences encourage the engagement of minds. This kind of programme is supported by Rosenham's (1969) study of the origins of concern for others. Voluntary rehearsal through training, as well as on-the-job interactions, can help the attitudes of prospective professionals to evolve more altruistically.

The prospective teachers' end-of-year superordinate constructs could help form the basis of an induction programme for their first year. Grant and Zeichner (1981) reported that carefully structured induction programmes are minimal or non-existent. Repertory grids may help better orient supervisors in relation to probationary or beginning teachers. Using their own lexicon could indicate their beginning views of, for example, themselves, pupils and administrators. This would allow for support to be personalized for them.

Present methods of statistical analysis of such perspectival changes are acknowledged as descriptive. Care needs also to be taken to ensure that explicit knowledge of development is not gained at the expense of personal validity. I sought the collaboration of the 17 teachers in seeking to construe their constructions, and 11 of them have been heard in their own voices. This helps prevent the guided tour from becoming too pale and ghostly a replica of the teachers' original exploratory experiences. Mode grids can suggest overlapping subjectivities and zones of understanding shared by a group of construers.

The comparison of successive matrices and grids helped focus the teachers' attention on how their constructions were transformed or remained unchanged. By exploring the personal principles of causality affecting the changes, they came to see themselves as full participants, able to use their unique positions as interpreters of their own perceptions. Bannister (1981) saw this capacity to self-reflect as both the source of a person's commentary on self and a central part of the experience of being a 'self'. Developing at least some understanding of how self-awareness develops and of the factors that may influence it is particularly crucial for teachers because the way that pupils learn to see themselves depends upon the way they believe that other people, and especially teachers, see them. Teachers thus need to reflect on the importance of their professional role in shaping the perspectives of pupils. By so doing they can monitor their own development and its effect on that of children. The Repertory grid is one way that teachers can focus on the formation and transformation of their points of view.

In the process of pre-service teacher education, where students are exposed to new ideas and to difficult, even traumatic situations, self-awareness is not simply important but even vital to their resolution. As Sonya concluded:

> I still feel so unready for next year. I feel so immature. Everyone else seems so much older or more experienced. I still feel like a learner rather than a teacher. I have a lot more learning to do. I want to make a

firm commitment to teaching but it's such a responsibility. At least I've learned to take a good look at myself.

In contrast, Sam, the teacher with the most consistently different perspective, realized that he had not really been either receptive to the course or committed to it. He had decided to teach in secondary school only until he could take up a full-time position as an Army instructor. Because some trainees expect to make teaching a life-time career, it may not provide their superordinate occupational constructs.

Though not claiming to have defined a universal pattern in intending teachers' perspectives, several overall trends have been usefully revealed, especially that of their final estrangement from pupils. The overall findings also endorse the notion that individual teachers' construction systems are unique and that, just as the content and organization differ from one to another, so too do the directions of the detailed changes. It is precisely this realization that led many of the intending teachers to report greater clarity in seeing and in recognizing themselves as altering, 'mental travellers' (William Blake, 1805).

It may be that transformation of perspective can take place only when individuals have sharper pictures of both what their actual teacher self and what their ideal looks like. As Sonya showed, by knowing what they are, they can form an idea of what they would like to be, and by knowing that, they can work towards it. In her last communication, Mitzi wrote:

> Everyone was looking for something different and went about adjusting to their particular perceived environments in different ways. However, the grid seemed to help most of us. To compare the three 'snapshots' of my year in DipEd has provided me with a much appreciated reflective experience. I came to terms with how as a person I felt about the prospect of teaching as a chosen career, what fears and anxieties I had in relation to teaching, as well as my perceptions of students. I came to see both what and how I saw.

When teachers are helped to 'open their eyes', they can see how to choose and fashion their own version of reality. By repacking their past for whatever needs arise, they can travel ahead psychologically in their own devices for observing and appraising.

Each teacher's own phrasebook and story

If a traveller is off to New England, New Orleans, New South Wales or New Zealand, a phrasebook or pocket guide is a useful purchase. Something similar needs to be made available to beginning teachers, and very early in their formal period of preparation. In pre-service teacher education, the strange land to be surveyed and explored is not the heavens but, even more challengingly, it is self as a teacher. The stranger the country we are visiting, the more threatening the prospect becomes. The more we realize that some degree of self-change may be involved, the more we must rely upon our own understanding of our own perspective and its potential advantages and limitations.

In order to choose which vision to pursue, beginning teachers need as much support and insight as possible. Helping them to reflect on the personal processes of how they experience the process of learning to teach helps them to experiment with and to change, in self-chosen ways, their own views of actual and imagined teaching practices. The phrasebook can be generated by examining their own developing repertoire of constructs so that, as a system of understanding, it presents them with both their own professional thesaurus of critical terms and their own teaching story. By learning to compose their own narratives, they can chart their way through their present and towards their future stages of development as teachers. 'Construct' itself as a term is appropriately ambiguous, capable of signifying not only construing or the process of construction but also its product, or that which is constructed.

Borthwick (1989) studied a second cohort of 17 intending teachers in the DipEd programme at the University of Queensland. These teachers confirmed that movement and change occurred both in the constructs they used on each of the three grid elicitation occasions and in the ways these constructs were structured. The findings support the view that, over the course of a single year, any change in constructs or transformation of perspective is unlikely either to be haphazard or to involve the sudden and total surrender of known repertoires for new ones. While the perspectival development of these teachers was gradual and evolutionary, they saw themselves as operating as personal scientists, able to use their existing constructs to predict their teaching behaviours and then, in the light of the consequences, to respond accordingly.

Writing in order to learn to teach

Like artists, beginning teachers can be shown to learn from the reflective study of their everyday activities. In addition to Repertory grid procedures, Diamond (1985a) and Borthwick (1989) used sustained writing programmes to help the individuals in the exploration of their experiences of the pre-service teaching year. As Salmon (1983, p. 92) also argued, an essential goal in teacher education is to help teachers to 'become present to themselves, so that they are able to engage with the material from their own personal standpoint' and to vary such engagements. Teacher educators can help by encouraging student teachers to reflect constantly upon and to dwell both in their own personal experience and in the concerns that shape it.

One route into this kind of personal explanation is through autobiographical practices so that teacher development is approached through the understandings teachers have of their own progress through schooling, higher education and student teaching. Teachers thus learn to foreground their own personal frameworks. To engage in study from the perspective of their continuing and future personal involvement in teaching requires the development of as full and intimate an understanding as possible of the personal stances that they can take towards becoming teachers. Teachers in their period of pre-service education need to be enabled to reflect personally and deeply upon their own present and future practice and what it may mean. Only a teacher education that is founded in our own experience can inform and keep flexible the standpoints from which we teach.

When the HMI (1987) survey of the initial training of teachers turned to written work, small-scale and individual investigations, simple research, practical work, teaching practice notebooks and dissertations were found. Competent expression and evidence of considerable background reading were evident. While there were few references to any uses of the teachers' self-narratives or autobiographies, the use of school-focused assignments was endorsed for developing effective links between the theory and practice of teaching. All of the professional and academic themes in one postgraduate certificate of education (PGCE) primary course were closely integrated with the beginning students' assignments. Assessments were based on journals that the students kept throughout the course and submitted periodically to their tutors. The introductory assignment related to the analysis of their first-hand experiences in school early in the course; and the second related to the theme of individual differences. These assignments were followed by an analysis of the initial teaching practice and then by an exercise related to the second theme of creativity and motivation. The assessment was completed by a report on team teaching in school and by work related to the final course theme of educational issues.

At worst, the HMI (1987) report on quality in British schools described methods in teacher education as themselves relying excessively on direct teaching where, because of shortage of time, expository methods were used too exclusively and student teachers were given too few opportunities to find out and think for themselves. A predominance of note-taking crowded out opportunities for discussion and the development of individual viewpoints. While the HMI allowed that another important element in a pre-service course involves the extent to which it can contribute to the personal, social and professional development of student teachers, the argument in the present book is that it is essential. While personal tutors could help co-ordinate other elements so that they are all fused into a cohesive offering, the recommended concern is not just with counselling and pastoral care but with reflection on the student's own development of perspective.

Teacher educators need to achieve a common appreciation and approach to cross-curricular issues such as provision of individual differences and development. Their own teaching can be informed by an appreciation of what the student teachers gather from the different parts of the course, both on campus and in the schools. Students like Mitzi and Grant often succumb to the school supervisors' methods rather than adapt those suggested by their university tutors when these approaches differ. A more secure relationship between different subjects and components in a course can be promoted by a fuller view of what the experience of learning to teach entails for individual student teachers.

Dow (1982) provided a planned and co-ordinated set of narrative contributions about teachers learning that was unified by the use of a credible, imaginary teacher and teaching situation. At the outset, the student as reader is introduced to Maria, a young teacher who has just started teaching (having taught elsewhere for a year) in a co-educational secondary school in a large industrial city. The school has very many students leaving school early and many from non-English-speaking backgrounds. A central theme of the narrative is that good teaching consists in making the best possible choices by weighing things up as they arise, that is, by developing habits of knowledgeable reflection, speculation and rationality, and not by settling mindlessly for a received store consisting of the truths of others.

In the DipEd course referred to by Diamond (1985a) and Borthwick (1989), the writing programme was designed to encourage individual reflection on the personal and shared experiences of learning to teach. Some of its suggested activities include:

- Write a letter to your tutor describing yourself as a learner.
- Interview a pupil or another student teacher during the practicum and provide a biographical sketch of him or her as a learner.
- Keep a personal record of your reading. List the books you read and describe your responses to them. 'As a teacher reading this book I found. . . .'
- What do you understand 'learning' to be? How does it relate to an individual person in process of, say, fashioning and refashioning meaning from the materials of experience?
- Do you learn by putting things in your own words? What else works for you?
- Complete the following or devise your own prompt to self-reflection:
  - 'I want to teach because. . . .'
  - 'On the first day of the practicum. . . .'
- What do you think makes for effective teaching? How well do you think you satisfy your own criteria of effective teaching? Reflect on your own teaching. How well did it satisfy the criteria of others, e.g. those of your pupils, supervising teachers, curriculum lecturers, and university or pastoral tutor?
- Devise a fable to represent your experiences of 'doing the DipEd'.
- Write an angry or happy short story about your learning to teach.

The aims of such writing is to enable different beginning teachers to take different paths and to learn about their own distinctive meaning systems, as well as the common perspectives they share. Each task provides an opportunity for them to structure the experiences of learning to teach, a chance to develop a distinctive lens through which to attend to their teaching. By being initiated into sense-making and by being able to thematize their own 'lived mindscapes' (Greene, 1984, p. 61), they can become challengers of their own present stories and involve themselves in self-critique. To reflect regularly upon their teaching situations is to try to understand some of the forces that frustrate their quests for themselves and their efforts to create themselves as the teachers they want to be. How successfully do you think Andrew is in coping with obstacles to his teacher development as dramatized in his following story?

An angry short story

Andrew spat disgustedly at the already moist pavement. 'What would they at the University know about anger?' he asked himself, putting his head back to stare distractedly at the clouds, jostling one another like stark grey cauliflowers in the sky. He drew his breath in sharply, and flicked his spent cigarette into the running gutter. He strode forcefully toward the library, slipped on the wet cement, regained his balance, and glanced around to make certain nobody had seen. He stuffed his hands in his pockets with a pout, and with a nonchalant slouch moved with careful, panther-like tread towards the swinging doors of the library. 'Angry? They think they were angry about the Secondary Prac.? They should have had to suffer mine!' Someone was coming through the swinging doors, and with a haughty side-step Andrew made way for him. He turned to enter, and the door swung back and caught him on the ankle.

Biting heavily on his cheek, Andrew swaggered towards the library steps. Yes, his secondary prac. was something to be angry about. His lips twisted in a bitter smile at the thought.

He had hoped – and he gave a rueful laugh to himself at the absurd naivete of the hope – that things would improve this time. That the school would be better, the teachers better organized, the classes better behaved. But of course it had all been an illusion. He could see that now.

He could see behind the smiling faces of the school staff to their benighted incompetence, could penetrate their superficial willingness and concern, could view with contempt their idle and ignorant souls.

Andrew bent at the drinking-fountain, opened his mouth over the jet and pressed the button. Nothing. He raised his head with an air of assumption, and closed his mouth.

But it was more than the schools which angered him. It was the whole disgraceful farce of the DipEd. They too had misled him, with their ingratiating smiles and their clever talk. They had perpetrated the lie – he could see that now – the lie that this could be a year of development and 'professional growth'.

Well, he had seen through that, had realized with savage conviction the falsity of their insidious propaganda. Professional growth? Pah! He barely checked himself from spitting on the worn puce of the library linoleum.

And he had been proven right. For all their talk, and for all the phoney sycophancy of the school-staff, no such growth had taken place. He had been right from the start, and his lip twitched with the scornful thought.

Andrew grunted as he pulled at the exit-door labelled 'Push'. He pushed the door open, and with a belligerent hunch made his way to the refec., where he would have a black coffee and another cigarette. It was a better place for him than the library, for he was *so* angry. And he was beginning to enjoy it.

This story and Andrew's self-characterization prompted further shared readings with other student teachers and raised significant questions that included: 'Who or what was spent in the practicum? What is the force of "pout" and "He could see that now"? What could Andrew see behind? Had any growth taken place? Does self-revelation or self-disclosure help to stretch our vision and expand our narrowing perspective?' Some other students also 'wrote' to Andrew by way of response and tested their experiences against his. Writing enables the transformation of knowledge structures, because it involves exactly that active effort to find connections that is central to learning. By writing we can discover what we know and adopt it into our frame of reference. Sometimes it requires that the perspective itself be adapted.

The transformation entailed in learning to teach starts with the exploration and articulation of the personal understandings that constitute a beginning teacher's perspective. For all those involved in trying to understand more fully these processes, the inquiry must involve their own personal contexts, their convictions and their own personal questions. As Salmon (1985, p. 125) wrote, it is the sense that we make of our teaching or of the way that we pay attention to it that 'gives the journey its direction, its sense of progression or development, its turning point, changes and passages, the meaning of its beginning and its end'.

4

In-service teacher education: countering contraction of perspective

Calderhead (1988b) described recent research in teacher education as suggesting that becoming and staying a teacher involves complex changes and development not only in teaching behaviour but also in cognition and emotion, and that these changes occur within powerful contexts. Conceptualization in teacher in-service education is generally fragmented and, consequently, there are only scattered bodies of research on teachers' belief systems, knowledge bases, classroom interaction, socialization, concerns, planning and problem solving, and on the translation of subject matter into teaching practice. In this chapter, a theoretical framework is provided to account for these different aspects of teacher development and to enable an overview of the complex processes and interactions that are involved in in-service teacher education.

In-service teacher education itself may be described very pragmatically and typically as any activity, usually deliberate and formalized, whereby teachers working beyond pre-service years may upgrade their professional understanding, skills and attitudes to broaden their perspectives. In-service education needs to help counter the contraction evident in teachers' perspectives when they feel that the premises with which they entered teaching are no longer useful and when they find that the classroom actions that arise from these premises no longer seem appropriate. They then need to learn to 'behold . . . the world, not univocally, but simultaneously through a set of prisms each of which catches some part of it' (Bruner, 1986, p. 25).

Many studies on the current impact of in-service or continuing education for teachers demonstrate that the process rarely produces positive outcomes. For example, the results of an early American review by Joyce *et al.* (1976) provided a discouraging account of many of the in-service programmes. The findings

reported were clearly negative, describing the courses as weak and impover-
ished and as relative failures. While Glassberg and Oja (1981) saw the major
source of difficulty in teacher education as the lack of coherent theory and
practice to promote teacher development, Eraut (1987) found that insufficient
account is taken of the teachers' predicament. In the present chapter, the gap
between the theory and the practice of teaching is bridged by applying Kelly's
(1955) theoretical constructs in the design and implementation of programmes of Fixed Role Treatment (FRT).

As an example of a growth rather than of a deficit approach, Oberg (1986)
found that using Kelly's theory yields a comprehensive picture of the personal
grounds of teacher practice. Making these grounds available for critical
examination by teachers raises the likelihood of improving practice. Once
teachers begin to view their teaching critically, they are likely to persist in
searching for ways of further improvement. Transformation of a teacher's
orientation towards his or her practice is a form of in-service education that has
'great potential for the transformation of educational practice in schools'
(Oberg, 1986, p. 64).

'They won't let me!'

Many researchers have painted poignant portraits of the lives of teachers as
they bravely attempt to influence the system in which they work. Strains and
frustrations foster burnout and, according to Shulman (1983, p. 502), 'an
insidious charing [may] slowly eat away at teacher(s)' in the performance of
their duties. Like their students (see Chapter 5), teachers often report a feeling
of exclusion, that school offers them little scope for personal choice or
individual initiative.

As Greene explained, it may be difficult for teachers to go beyond present
procedures and arrangements. Confronted with schooling structures and
political pressures, many come to learn to cope 'by becoming merely efficient,
by functioning compliantly – like Kafkaesque clerks' (Greene, 1978, p. 28).
While some may protect themselves by remaining basically uninvolved, others
may become so bored and so lacking in any prospect that they no longer care.
Lacking awareness of their own personal realities they cannot relate to students
and become unwitting accomplices of an inequitable system. Lacking a sense of
self they sit back and affirm that they are constrained and defined by their
teaching roles. The habit becomes one of blaming ineffectiveness upon
circumstances and institutions, one of blaming others rather than oneself.
Failures are focused on, rather than successes. However, our experiences of
ourselves as teachers have meaning for us not only in terms of our historically
situated consciousness but also in terms of our personally located consciousness (Smyth, 1989b).

When the construct systems of 15 teachers, relating to the teaching of composition, were studied in the process of being implemented, numerous gaps were found to open up within their perspectives, that is, between their intentions and actions (Diamond, 1982a). However, actual obstruction in the area of instruction could so rarely be attributed to school administrators that the teachers may not reasonably blame 'them' for the chains they seem to wear. Why is it that teachers imprison themselves? The findings raised the uncomfortable possibility that teachers themselves might be determining that their fate be thought of as already determined, that is, that they might be digging the very graves that they claim are threatening to swallow them up. But there may be worse to come if teachers dare to step outside and go beyond the safe and familiar perspectives on teaching. Venturing to find new avenues of freedom they may reap considerable distress. It may prove to be too audacious for them, living on the frontiers of personal experience rather than remaining trapped within cosily settled conventions as the self-martyring victims of the demands of others. As William James illustrated, it is stressful having to break out afresh. In a railroad accident a circus tiger, whose cage had broken open, is said to have emerged, but then crept back again, 'as if too much bewildered by his new responsibilities, so that he was without difficulty secured' (James, 1892, p. 10).

In order to accept the invitation to assume personal responsibility for venturing abroad, teachers need to learn to recognize threats and then to develop ways of coping with them. When they experience a strong sense of external pressure, they need to recognize that, as Bakan (1974) suggested, this may be illusory and in fact only the projection of their own internal fears. Instead of reacting repeatedly with rigid patterns, teachers may need to react more vividly to the actual experiences according to their specific nature. This kind of fixity or the feeling of being 'struck' is the psychological cost of having lost the sense of search and the sense of the freshness of experience. Teachers need to see themselves as self-fashioning beings who can make themselves into what they want to be. But how can they learn to grow in self-determined directions and play better parts? How can transformation be sought?

Within Kelly's (1955, p. 15) assumption that 'all of our present interpretations of the universe are subject to revision and replacement' lies hope that teachers too can change. They will be more likely to give up a viewpoint, even if it is one that is an integral part of themselves, if they can become aware of the personally meaningful implications of the alternative perspective that, in this instance, is to be more self-determining and effective. Teachers need to be helped to forge personally effective, alternative approaches.

Slow to change

As I puzzled over the paradoxical situation of teachers' self-invented powerlessness, I remembered our first Christmas in London (Diamond, 1982b). Just before breakfast we found that the oven would not heat up. 'What about the thawed turkey? What about dinner?' Later I began wondering what it would take to convince me to become a vegetarian. I could read about alarming increases in degenerate diseases and perhaps be persuaded that they could be halved by simple changes in diet. Perhaps 'genuine case histories' (see Chapter 6) could help prepare for my dietary conversion, leading finally to a transformative belief in natural healing through macrobiotics. But, apart from a defective stove or an empty larder, what would prompt me to seek energetically an effective alternative to my present conventional dietary understandings? I began to worry about what friends would think. Would they still extend dinner invitations? Why should I take the trouble to change? Fortunately, the caretaker showed us how to return the stove's control to manual and we enjoyed the planned dinner, eventually. But the question relating to slow change remained to be answered.

If there is only anxiety and threat out there, no change is likely to eventuate. Rather than invoking moral condemnations, it has to be realized that change is possible for all of us only when there is some understanding of an alternative. Raphael (1976, p. 56) is too coldly rational in *The Glittering Prizes* when he insists that 'one does not replace a lie, nor does one need to have a replacement in order to show that it is one. Nonsense is not replaced, it is simply eliminated.' In pedagogy, as in diet or arguments, no-one voluntarily risks conceptual confusion or even the anguish of chaos by merely relinquishing life-long professional beliefs. No-one takes the extra trouble. If movement is to occur, it is only possible when there is a framework within which it may take place. In addition, the more meaningful one way of teaching or behaving has become, as opposed to its unknown alternatives, the more difficult it is to change that perspective.

If the prospects of a meatless Christmas stirred novel thoughts of vegetarianism, turkey tartare never suggested itself! Somewhat more empirically, Crockett and Meisel (1974) have shown that change is especially difficult when central, highly implicatory constructs are involved. People are loath to change in any way that entails too many related changes. The prospect of massive linked changes is too daunting. In addition, if a construct system is only weakly disconfirmed as in the failure of only one meal, little or no response may be made. On the other hand, if an inference on a central or superordinate construct can be directly and strongly refuted, transformation may occur. Like collapsing dominoes, once change occurs in a highly connected system, change is greater among the interrelated constructs than among the independent, peripheral ones. If constructs are segmented or only sparsely pyramided, relatively few changes follow disconfirmation even of the most central and nuclear constructs.

Ineffective pedagogy

When the practice of a group of 15 teachers was studied for a school year, none was found to be able to promote significant overall gains in whole class achievement in, or in attitudes towards, personal and expository writing (Diamond, 1979). When the teachers were subsequently re-interviewed, not one of them disputed these disturbing findings but rather all accepted them stoically as representing the way things really are during the last year of compulsory schooling. One teacher admitted, 'By the end of the second semester their work in English had fallen away', and another reported, 'I discussed the decline with other teachers and they agreed that it appears in their classes too.' A third teacher agreed movingly that the lack of effectiveness accorded with her own experiences of the year: 'I can say with mine that in the last half of the year that I had a very negative effect on them because I just "lost it" and I know the class did too. There was nothing I could do.' There is such self-deprecation in these remarks that one wonders how some teachers seem to be running so fast and not even have their classes stay on the same spot in regard to written performance. It is a mystery how their construct systems continue to survive unchanged.

A Kellyian perspective

Three structural explanations are possible as to why many teachers may be unable decisively to test out and elaborate their personal theories, in this case, of writing instruction. First, their construing may have become circular so that they endlessly test and retest the same hypotheses (for example, 'teach the skills in isolation') and are thus unable to accept the disquieting implications of the data they collect. Secondly, the teachers may have moved into the kind of chaos where constructions are so vague and loose (for example, 'teach for feelings and personal growth') that they cannot provide expectations clear enough to be tested, and so simply circle and recircle around the same issues, projecting the feeling that 'they won't let me!' Thirdly, they may have moved, by contrast, in the direction of total constriction (for example, 'nothing works'), as events refuse to comply with their rigid prediction. Such closed construct systems are unable to deal with invalidating evidence and represent a state of psychosclerosis or of hardening of the categories.

The second explanation suggests that teachers have experienced invalidation so frequently that they eventually begin to loosen the linkages between their constructs to such a degree that specific predictions are no longer generated. One teacher, for example, explained that 'You just don't see growth with a lot of kids. They may try a bit harder or just become a lot happier in your room. But that doesn't mean that their writing improves. They're better as people, that's all.' Invalidity may be avoided but at the cost of teaching almost entirely in a fluid and largely meaningless universe. This loosening or dis-integration may help explain why teaching has been viewed as essentially pre-theoretical, providing a sensate, existential knowledge of a purely concrete nature that eludes theoretical explanations. Using his own researcher perspective, Jackson (1968) described even outstanding teachers as 'here-and-now' oriented, instinctive rather than reflective, people of action and feeling rather than of control and thought. Theirs was a so-called conceptual simplicity, allegedly revealed in an uncomplicated view of causality, in an intuitive rather than rational approach to classroom events, and in an opinionated rather than a 'wait-and-see' stance towards alternative teaching practices. One of my rep-resentative teachers commented, 'I honestly don't think teachers go around in their heads and separate those ideas out. Your ordinary, run of the mill, classroom teacher doesn't break it down.' Another explained, 'Often a lot of things you do don't make much impact, depending on the type of student you have. . . . Really there's not much we can do. It all depends on the kind of home they come from.' However, teachers may be doing much well that is not captured by the researcher's own limited perspective.

While findings such as these do not provide warrant for rejecting teachers' personal and practical knowledge as second-class, they do provide some ground for accepting the scenario wherein people who are faced with repeated invalidation of parts of their construct systems first of all alter the pattern of relationships between their constructs (in effect, repeatedly altering their pedagogic theory in an eclectic, wildly oscillating fashion), but eventually begin to loosen the relationships between their constructs and in effect start to abandon the theory-holding business. It may be that a central role for in-service teacher educators is to let themselves be used by teachers so that the teachers can then learn to validate themselves and thus form their own pedagogical relationships and perspectives. The challenge is to help teachers to see themselves as self-directing and self-determining, as professionally competent and as capable of trying alternative pedagogies. The required rethinking may not merely 'recalibrate what we already do but [may] carry us considerably beyond where we are now' (Smyth, 1989a, p. 165).

Fixed role treatment

Day (1984) argued that research and in-service teacher education can make significant contributions if the researchers and teacher educators learn to move away from seeing themselves as the prime designers and interpreters of teachers' thoughts and actions towards a more interdependent role in which collaboration, consultation and negotiation are first principles. In his model of classroom-based in-service education, four teachers had sequences of lessons filmed and the videos then discussed at length in order to generate more personal, pedagogical theory through reflection and deliberation. The teachers reported that they came to trust more their own ability not only to find but also evaluate and modify their own solutions to the teaching problems they encountered. In this way, Day (1984) became a part of rather than apart from the teachers. He assumed a model of teachers who, given particular circumstances, are able to distance themselves from the world in which they are everyday participants and open themselves to rational influence by others. This distancing is an essential first step towards self-evaluation. Distancing and self-evaluation help define perspective expansion or transformation. Smyth (1989a) insisted that what is needed for such an alternative vision is less measurement against standards of performance and more activity of an ethnographic, biographical and autobiographical kind.

Teachers' stable patterns of perception, interpretation and action may need to be breached in order to rescue their constructs from the immunity of long-term invalidation. Change can begin by their looking for alternative interpretations of classroom events. By becoming aware of their bondage to routines, teachers can then dare to search out new hypotheses. Helping teachers as learners to gain access to alternative meaning perspectives for interpreting reality is central to transformation. Different perspectives such as those of the student, those of the researcher or those of the teachers themselves at different stages in their careers, can be presented with their different implications to counter such contraction. In-service education needs to help release teachers from the imprisonment of contracted perspectives. Picasso with his portraits, Hockney with his photographs and Barthes with his self-narratives have exploded perspectives to subvert the tyranny of the traditional one-point perspective and to permit movement into a world of multiple perspectives.

Uccello, an early Renaissance painter, was intoxicated with the subject of perspective and established new means of rendering it. His painting of 'The Flood and the Recession of the Flood' was shown by Phillipson (1989) as giving two perspectival images within the 'one' pictorial space. The artist's reflexive turn from the outside back on to and into self leads towards the space of an inner flood in which stable spatial and temporal reference points are collapsed. In a similar way, the possibility of teachers' self-transforming relations with their own pedagogy seems bound to the rhythms of their writing and reading about it and to their shifting from the comfort of remaining a mundane teacher self to the challenge of becoming the teacher they would like to be. This movement may also be described as transformation of perspective. It too can be courted by a plunge into their own inner floods or streams of consciousness to test boundaries and their own 'delimiting possibilities' (Phillipson, 1989, p. 8).

Self-characterization

Kelly (1955) proposed that people choose between alternative roles that are defined for them by their personal constructs. These constructs constitute implicit networks or systems on which people structure their thinking in order to view their own behaviour and that of others. People are paradoxically both controlled and set free by their viewpoints, and, in order to choose which role they will play, they need to be more aware of possible variations. Kelly proposed several techniques that could be used to investigate these personal constructs and to induce change; Fixed Role Therapy or Treatment (FRT) is one of them.

Little research has been documented using Kelly's FRT, particularly in teaching. In other fields, research is also limited: Karst and Trexler (1970) used this approach to treat anxiety associated with public speaking; Bonarius (1970) presented a case study showing the phases involved in the role change of a patient; and Radley (1974) proposed that role enactment might be a formalized reflection of the constructive processes by which people are able to make explicit their construct roles in order then to choose between them.

Diamond (1983b) provided a case study of FRT devised to help change the construct systems underlying the classroom pedagogies of two high school English teachers. The teachers, to be called Fay and Ann, were volunteers from a large suburban high school. Fay was 22 years of age, a 4-year university-trained teacher of 2 years experience; Ann was 20 years of age, a 3-year college-trained teacher in her first year of teaching. Both had very limited experience of teaching English. Only Ann had been trained specifically to teach it.

The teachers were invited to provide a 500-word professional self-description of how they perceived themselves as English teachers. The initial instructions were:

> I want you to write a teaching sketch of Julie Brown, just as if she were the principal character in a play. Write it as it might be written by a friend and professional colleague who knows her INTIMATELY and very SYM-PATHETICALLY, perhaps better than anyone could know her. Be sure to write it in the third person. For example, start out by saying:
> 'As a teacher, Julie Brown is. . . .'

Each teacher substituted her own name for the mythical Brown. Kelly chose the words carefully so that 'sketch' suggested that general structure, rather than elaborate detail, was to be described. This meant that the teachers' central and interrelated constructs or perspectives were to be revealed. Emphasis on the third person indicated that it was not to be a chronicle of faults or virtues, but a view of the whole teacher. The other phrases sought to reduce any threat and to encourage the production of speculation as well as facts.

Both self-characterizations were shared with me as the teacher educator for diagnostic and textual analyses of the teachers' pedagogical construct systems. I then devised role character sketches centring on alternative teaching styles for the teachers. These protagonists bore the fictitious names of Carole Spencer and Jill Hartley, respectively. Of course, if a teacher perspective is to be changed, more than a mere change in name is required. But the name change, together with the other terms of the new teaching identity, can have deep psychological and pedagogical implications.

The scenarios were designed to be sympathetic to and to fit the teaching situations confronting each of the teachers. Each was encouraged to become the teacher outlined in the sketch in every way possible for a limited time. For five consecutive teaching days, they attempted to construe and teach as these other teachers. The period of enactment for Fay preceded that for Ann by one week. One interview to monitor progress was held between Fay and myself. Ann was given feedback only through subsequent discussions with Fay. Student reactions were observed by the teachers themselves.

In order to produce the self-characterizations, the teachers had to relate the facts as they related to themselves. They produced personal self-diagnoses, within the frameworks of their own pedagogical construct systems. By examining the sketches, I saw at least partially how their construct systems had enabled them to paint themselves into corners so that they were virtually stuck. Clinical methods of analysing the sketches were provided by Kelly (1955) and by Bannister and Fransella (1986). As shown in Chapter 7 my analysis also took the form of a storying response.

Fay's first sentence was 'Fay feels there are many areas of concern in her own teaching methods and content which need attention', and her last sentence, 'Her lessons seem to be dull and uninteresting and time consuming.' Being a better, more efficient and interesting teacher seemed to be emphasized as her major teaching construct. Ann's first sentence was 'Ann is still finding her feet', and her last sentence, 'Most importantly she has to be determined to improve herself and overcome these problems in order to help herself and, of course, her students.' This teacher's major construct seemed to emerge as struggling to find out for herself versus being told the right answers.

The most important requirement of the role sketch was that the main perspective implied by the role would be different from, or at 90 degrees to, that of the teacher. Fay's sketch (Carole Spencer) was written around the relatively simple theme of enjoying her own contributions and those of her students, rather than being policed by people in authority. Ann's sketch (Jill Hartley) explored not settling passively for the 'right' answers as supplied by others, but rather searching out her own through active collaboration with her students. The tone of each sketch was positive; for example, 'Of course not everything works – just most of it!'

The two self-characterizations were then thematically analysed by searching each of them for key words and phrases, and by then assembling a rough classification or structuration. Fay and Ann shared two recurring themes: 'difficulty' and 'how to'. They had a common view of teaching as a difficult and pragmatic activity. Fay repeated three other themes in her teaching self-portrait: 'concern (areas of)', 'students' and 'time-waste'. Ann used six other themes to delineate her teaching self: 'interest', 'motivation', 'find out', 'herself' 'problems' and 'suggestions'. Though Fay seemed to focus on her students, and Ann, a teacher in her first year, on herself, Ann was also very much concerned with interesting and motivating her students.

This thematic analysis confirmed that Fay's alternative sketch should stress enjoying being with her students, rather than focusing on time-waste and efficiency (see Chapter 1). Also, she was encouraged to put activity before generalized anxiety. Similarly, Ann's sketch should stimulate her to form a languaging community with her students, rather than seeking alternately to beguile them with interest and motivation and then to discipline them with assessment. The sketches also included specific 'how to' activities in order to meet both teachers' more pragmatic needs.

Fay seemed to be more successful than Ann in assuming her role character, and she showed greater apparent change or transformation in her personal constructs of teaching English. She was no longer 'stuck'. While reported student reaction did not favour either of them, some promising responses came from two of Fay's classes.

Fay's self-reported changes included increased awareness of alternative teaching strategies, feelings of greater self-understanding and self-confidence, decreased tension, and a desire to continue to explore areas in teaching previously considered unsafe. In contrast, Ann confessed to feelings of threat and anxiety when faced with the prospect of using the alternative methods. She felt that the coping mechanisms she had established at the beginning of the year were still working adequately for her. This was particularly so with a class of year 10 boys who posed constant discipline problems for her. Although Ann was aware of her own ability to change her perspectives, she still expected some kind of external deliverance. With one class, however, Ann felt that her alternative teaching role would have been successful if only assessment had not been required by her head of department just at that time. As a first-year teacher, she registered a strong sense of external demand.

Both teachers volunteered to elaborate their 'troubles' in teaching English before and after their periods of role enactment. Such exercises can progressively confront teachers with alternatives and involve them in the creativity cycle of loosening and tightening of perspectives. Fay's 'pre-test' included:

THE TROUBLE WITH TEACHING ENGLISH IS I don't seem to know where I'm going – I feel confused. There seems to be no overall pattern for me. TEACHING ENGLISH IS LIKE THAT because I was never trained and have had to learn by my mistakes. ANOTHER REASON IS THAT I don't seem to get any feedback about how and what I teach. IT WOULD BE BETTER IF I could find out exactly where I was going in teaching English. That would make a lot of difference to me, to feel confident.

In contrast, her 'post-test' consisted of:

THE TROUBLE WITH TEACHING ENGLISH IS now limited or it seems less anyway. I feel better – less worried. I'm getting used to being different. TEACHING ENGLISH IS LIKE THAT BECAUSE I feel better within myself. ANOTHER REASON IS THAT teaching English is also more rewarding than it used to be. IT WOULD BE BETTER IF I used more of the techniques outlined for me more of the time. It made a difference to me because I'm happier, more relaxed and more aware – even a bit wiser!

As Kelly (1969) suggested, FRT is an iconclastic venture that involves placing oneself in new relationships. Fay's confusion, lack of knowledge and overall pattern were replaced by her being less worried, and by feeling better, more relaxed and aware.

In contrast, Ann recorded less movement. Her 'pre-test' included:

THE TROUBLE WITH TEACHING ENGLISH IS the lack of a basic content guideline. What to teach and what levels should be expected are also vague. TEACHING ENGLISH IS LIKE THAT BECAUSE it is an abstract subject with a need for a wide general knowledge. ANOTHER REASON IS a need to be able to teach and have general understanding of a variety of personalities and levels. IT WOULD BE BETTER IF more guidance was given in actual teaching circumstance. WHAT DIFFERENCE WOULD THAT MAKE? . . .

Her 'post-test' consisted of:

THE TROUBLE WITH TEACHING ENGLISH NOW IS learning and under-standing new methods fully enough for the lesson to be a success. TEACHING ENGLISH IS LIKE THAT BECAUSE students expect a certain thing from English, dependent on past teachers and experiences. ANOTHER REASON IS assessment can override time and new thoughts and programmes. IT WOULD BE BETTER IF a more convenient time for changing teaching strategies could be found. At the right time of year with the right class these could bring about more successful differences.

Few changes seem to have been accomplished by Ann: students, assessment and the time of year were not right for her. She still wanted more guidance, and had not experienced the benefits of becoming self-directing.

Fay seems to have been more successful as a result of adopting her role character. She had previously felt very confused and frustrated when teaching English, possibly through either lack of school direction or lack of training and experience. At times these misgivings were still experienced, but, as her elaboration of teaching troubles showed, there had been improvements. She reported feeling the need to be more adventurous, despite the possibility of failure and temporary disorganization in class. She was using, she said, 'Nothing ventured, nothing gained' as her teaching motto. In addition, Fay seemed to worry less about her success as a teacher, realizing that each lesson could be a limited venture, without her whole teaching career being at stake.

By becoming more attuned to the relevance for her pupils of what she taught, Fay noted a paradoxical increase in her own self-understanding. This, however, may have been due not only to the changed teaching strategies and her self-examination, but also to her discussions with another teacher at her school who had a 'functional approach to teaching language'. This viewpoint made sense after she observed a poetry lesson taught by this teacher that featured students reading poems out loud, using their own facial and vocal expressions. This was seen as a great success, and helped to reconcile the competing claims of school assessment and student involvement. Fay was led to try similar activities in her own class. In contrast, not all the techniques embodied in the alternative teaching scenario worked for Fay, but she was beginning to make her own choices. Her tensions had been released by the wide range of possible teaching strategies that had been suggested to her.

Fay welcomed the increased self-confidence that she experienced after seeing some of the alternatives work for her. She still felt that other changes were needed, such as increased class interest, variety in activities and more relaxed talk in her lessons. She realized that these changes would take more time than the present study could encompass. She felt that even closer monitoring of her lessons by me as the teacher educator would have been helpful.

Fay had originally sought to help to change her pedagogy, and once her FRT was launched, she had offered a similar opportunity to Ann. This second teacher, however, failed to report increased feelings of satisfaction and self-confidence as a result of the FRT. She continued to be reluctant to try the new teaching strategies that had been suggested. She felt extremely limited by her classes. The non-academic class of boys rigidly resisted any alteration to their routine. Another class that would have been more responsive to change was caught up in assessment procedures required of all the year 11 classes. Her year 8 class had successfully completed an autobiography in school time. This was not set as homework and had helped to break the punitive link between writing and impositions. However, Ann still saw this class as unsettled and requiring close supervision.

Ann found it difficult to attempt some of the suggestions with her two year 10 classes, because she could not justify to herself expending the effort that this would have entailed. These classes were due to leave school in 4 weeks, and she was intent on surviving her first year. She was afraid to negotiate a truce with these school leavers. For her, it was the wrong time of year with the wrong classes.

An important factor in Fay's comparatively greater transformation of perspective may have been her having voluntarily sought out help to plunge into her teacher self. As Kelly (1955) noted, some changes of one sort or another can be expected to follow such action, regardless of whether or not the help itself materializes. Fay's very conception of herself as a teacher 'on the move' and undertaking a FRT carried with it certain implications that were likely to bring about a series of positive revisions in her teaching. Seeking change is itself an event of some significance. As Ann writes, the best thing teachers can do is first to realize that they may have problems. They then need to review their synoptic views of teaching.

Repertory grid

Ingvarson and Greenway (1984) used a Repertory grid approach to describe the career biographies of two teachers and to represent their experience and development from the inside. The value of the method is that it displays graphically the content of the teachers' outlooks, revealing the intricate connections between their ideals and the mundane features of their teaching life, their aspirations and their career realities. The ease with which other teachers may generalize from such case studies to their own teaching indicates that such portrayals can touch on elements common to the experience of many teachers.

Pablo the chess player in Herman Hesse's (1929) *Steppenwolf* offers instructions in the build-up of personality or perspective. This requires that he be given the pieces into which the so-called personality can be broken. Pablo then magically transforms the pieces into characters in successive scenes where they enact their own worlds. He adds that this is the art of life. 'You may yourself as an artist develop the game of your life and lend it animation. You may complicate and enrich it as you please. It lies in your hands' (Hesse 1929, p. 215). So too in teacher in-service. The effort is not to give the teacher the right answer, which often has meant getting the teacher's construct system to conform to that of the teacher educator or researcher. Rather, the process is considered as an occasion for learning, for testing the fit of one's own construct system and the position of teacher self within it. To do this, a kind of role-playing approach is employed, much in the spirit of characters in a Pirandello play, who learn of themselves partly through the experience of contrasting or confusing (or both) what they are with the mask they are wearing in different life situations. They can explore the relationship between the teachers they are and those they want to be.

Teaching in these terms is simply another aspect of life to be examined and then confirmed or corrected. Because constructs not only represent a person's private view of reality but also set limits beyond which the person finds it difficult to perceive, personal constructs enable and constrain, facilitate and restrict a person's range of action. People regularly invent theories, any one of which is as much a psychological venture as a logical entity. Even people's most familiar constructs are not objective observations of what is really there, but are instead their present 'best projections'. For Kelly (1970), there are simply too many ways of explaining the same facts – including a lot of ways that have not turned up yet – for anyone to claim privileged communication with either God or nature.

A sharply contrasting philosophical view insists that there is 'one way' and defers to a master plan for mankind, with people comprising a conforming theatrical group with their roles preordained according to some shadowy, pre-existing script. However, it may be that people are not involved with a predetermined script on a preset stage but are part of a constant improvisation in which each member of the troupe must be a spontaneous actor, playwright, member of the audience and critic. The parts are neither prescribed nor assigned. Forgotten lines, miscues, late entries and hasty exits are inevitable, yet an infinite number of combinations await the players. In such an open system, errors must occur, but people are not bound to them because they are able successively to correct them.

There is considerable psychological interest in such abstract knowledge structures as perspectives. Teachers can be hypothesized to articulate their constructs in the form of scripts to produce conceptual representations of teaching events. FRT is then used as an educational procedure rather than a therapeutic method and begins with the identification of the teachers' individual constructs (perhaps as embodied in such a sequence) and seeks their review or transformation through a process of alternative role enactment. Kelly has provided a number of techniques that can be used first to detect the components that comprise a personality, then to promote experimentalism, and finally to achieve reconstruction. Dialogue is a feature of these techniques. In this respect, FRT is not intrinsically different from everyday activities, because everyone seeks to understand themselves and others. They routinely elicit the constructs of others in conversation and discussion.

FRT is a means of countering contraction of perspective that is based upon the effects of dramatic experience. Although role-playing is a behavioural change procedure used by many theorists with a variety of orientations, FRT is different from psychodrama, for example, in that it emphasizes rehearsing new behaviours to be used in the future. FRT traditionally begins with people being requested to write out their taken-for-granted teaching scripts in the third person (see Diamond, 1983b). In the next study (Diamond, 1985b), the self-characterizations were gathered not through verbal self-reports but from the ways in which teachers used their personal constructs to describe centrally important elements in a Repertory grid involving people and teaching. The portrayals of the *teacher I am*, the *teacher I would like to be* and *pupils* were used to devise alternative role sketches that invited the teachers to explore either contrasting or confirmatory teaching behaviours. Major teaching themes were developed rather than seeking the correction of minor difficulties. The counter-script sought to set the stage for the resumption or the continuation of growth, movement and change. The teachers were encouraged to review or reformulate the perspectives underlying their classroom pedagogies.

Fifteen teachers studying in a university Bachelor of Education Studies undertook the FRT. The intact group consisted of eight men and seven women. Seven of them were teaching in primary, five in secondary and three in further education. Eleven had been teaching for over 4 years and 11 had taught without a career interruption.

I explained that the purpose of the study was to enable them to confirm or reorganize their views of people and teaching. The 'pre-' and 'post-tests' each took about 2 hours to complete and consisted of a shortened, modified group version of Kelly's Role Construct Repertory Grid. Fifteen figures, considered to be some of the major human elements in teaching, were used as the elements (see Table 5). A specific person had to be thought of to fit each role description. The triads were randomly selected and 12 comparison sortings were required.

The revised form was faithful to Kelly's original procedures. The teachers had to build their constructs around specific people representative of their own teaching lives. The figures include six self and personal teacher references, family members, friends, administrators and pupils. The constructs were elicited as above by the triadic sorting of the elements into the two that were *similar* (emergent pole) and the one that was *different* in meaning (implicit). The constructs were then used to represent a 5-point scale ranging from the emergent (1) to the implicit (5) pole. All the elements were subsequently rated on all the constructs.

We examined the descriptions together of the *teacher I am*, the *teacher I would like to be* and *pupils* to see if individual teachers had so constrained themselves that they were unable to move. I then drew up for each of them a

Table 5   Role title list (in-service)

Figure number	Figure description
1	Self
2	Past self
3	Ideal self
4	Teacher I am
5	Teacher I fear to be
6	Teacher I would like to be
7	Mother
8	Father
9	Siblings
10	Spouse/steady
11	Friends
12	Pupils
13	Principal and deputy
14	Subject master
15	Inspector

portrait of another teacher who was somewhat different from the original teacher's pedagogical self-portrait. Each teacher was then asked to play the teacher described in this sketch and not someone who was totally and dramatically opposite. For example, if the teacher had taught the skills in isolation, he or she was asked not to totally ignore them but rather to teach them in context. The aim was to help the teachers find new dimensions or perspectives along which to view teaching and not merely to slot-rattle along the old ones, as, for example, from 'chicken to eagle', from 'struggling to superstar', or from 'didactic teaching to radical non-interference'. Nor were the teachers to move just to mid- or so-called 'balanced' points. The sketches involved the teachers in new but not too demanding ventures and only their roles were 'on the line'.

By way of an acceptance check, the created role character was shared with each teacher who was asked if such a teacher was credible, not too threatening and even likeable. If not, it was altered until those criteria were met. The teacher was then asked to 'be' the fictitious teacher for 10 consecutive days in the classroom. The teacher kept a copy of the script, read it at least three times a day and tried to teach, think and talk like the other teacher. The teacher was to set the kinds of assignments such an imagined teacher would devise, do that teacher's kinds of personal planning, read books and articles, respond to students' questions and productions and seek to interpret lessons entirely from that teacher's perspective. I emphasized that this was only a limited experiment and at the conclusion of the time the teacher would revert to his or her own teaching identity. The new role was neither an ideal nor a panacea but merely an hypothesis – an invitation to reconstruct. During the trial period of enactment, the teacher and I met to discuss how the role was being interpreted and received. The teacher was also encouraged to keep a diary or growth map during this time. The Repertory grid was finally repeated to monitor any changes in perspectives.

The FOCUS computer program was used as in Chapter 3 to analyse each grid. The relationships were visualized as tree diagrams for the constructs and the elements that showed the highest similarities in the clusters. The SOCIOGRIDS program was used to analyse the set of two Repertory grids elicited from each teacher (before and after the fixed role enactment). The PAIRS algorithm computed the measure of similarity between each two grids to provide a measure of movements. SOCIOGRIDS was used also to explore the similarity and differences in construing between the groups of teachers. The program analysed the set of Repertory grids elicited from the group on each occasion and based similarity in terms of the ordering of the element set. Two mode grids were extracted for the group and in each case the number of modal constructs was comparable to the number of constructs in the separate individual grids. SOCIOGRIDS was used finally to compare the two mode grids and to detect the amount of group change.

When each teacher's two grids were compared, as shown by the summary in

Table 6   Grid similarity, pre- to post-test

Grid no.	1	2	3	4	5	6	7	8	9	10	11	12	13	14	15
Teacher ID	01	03	04	06	08	09	10	11	12	16	18	19	20	21	22
%	71	61	66	72	68	82	82	63	66	82	68	70	74	75	68

Table 6, teachers 03, 11, 04 and 12 were salient in most having changed their perspectives. This was indexed by the low overall similarity of their respective grids (61, 63, 66 and 66 percent). Teachers 09, 10 and 16 were conversely prominent, because their perspective had changed the least.

After each individual teacher had his or her 'pre-' and 'post-test' mapping of the area of people and teaching FOCUS-ed and contrasted, a mode or group grid of the constructs most commonly used by all the teachers on each occasion was extracted and then focused in order to show the content of the group's shared construing. Each construct in the two mode grids was derived from a teacher in the group so that the mode grids were not consensus grids that averaged out the individualities, but were instead strongly weighted towards the commonality of construing within the group.

In the 'pre-test' mode grid three major clusters appeared at the 70 percent level. There was a high degree of emphasis on the following superordinate constructs: (1) same ideas/different values; loving, gentle/immature; and warm, caring/distant; (2) sensitive/insensitive; humanitarian/unambitious; open, tactful/labile; and insightful/introverted; and (3) hardworking/delegates unfairly; friendly/aggressive; and calm/excitable. Constructs 1 and 6, loving, gentle/immature and same ideals/different values, were most highly matched at the 90 percent level.

In the 'post-test' mode grid two more tightly knit clusters were found at the 80 percent level. These superordinates consisted of: (1) other regard/self regard; love/dislike children; sensitive/insensitive; and thoughtful/thoughtless; and (2) warm interest/reserve quiet; warm, genuine/authoritarian; friendly/lacking encouragement; and rational/irrational. A major and continuing concern of the teachers was with warm, loving and humanitarian relationships. When the two mode grids were compared, they remained associated at the 81 percent level.

In the teachers' 'pre-test' clustering of elements, the *teacher I am* was most closely linked in a family circle, with *self, friends, mother* and *past self*, while *pupils* were located in a school group together with *principal* and *deputy, subject master* and *inspector*. In the 'post-test' element tree, the *teacher I am* was linked once again with *self* and *friends* but now also very intimately with *pupils* at the 93 percent level. Before the role enactment, the *teacher I am* had been related with *pupils* only at the 66 percent level.

The *teacher I am* was initially seen as extremely like other teachers in aims and ideals, loving and gentle, warm and caring, sensitive, humanitarian, insightful, hardworking, friendly and calm. *Pupils* were also depicted as sensitive and humanitarian, open and tactful, but not as hardworking, and extremely aggressive and excitable. The teachers were then undecided where the *pupils* could be located on half the shared dimensions.

After the role enactments, the *teacher I am* came to be described as having regard for others, loving children, sensitive, thoughtful, hardworking, warm, interested and genuine, friendly and jovial, rational and independent. The *pupils* were then more widely and positively appreciated in terms of 10 of the qualities attributed to people and teaching. They were felt to be sensitive, thoughtful, hardworking, warm, interested and genuine, friendly and jovial, rational, independent and easy going. Like the teachers, they had come to be recognized as similar in their own group interests. Perceptions of the *pupils* were transformed in that they were finally acknowledged as hardworking and no longer as extremely aggressive. Also, the teachers seemed to be less sure of, and to question more, their own notions of their past pedagogic selves. Teacher 04, for example, was particularly anxious to avoid regressing to his former cold, bureaucratic and distant self.

While teachers 03, 11, 04 and 12 were shown to have most changed their perspectives and teachers 09, 10 and 16 the least, FRT seems to have promoted the personal and professional transformation of most of the teachers because, suggestibility aside, the mode degree of association between the *teacher I am* and *pupils* was dramatically improved from 66 to 93 percent. Teacher 12's attitudes towards *pupils*, for example, showed just such a positive change. In her 'pre-test' element matrix, they were closely related to *teacher I fear to be* and *past self* but not to *ideal self* and *teacher I would like to be*. However, in her 'post-test' element matrix, *pupils* were related to *self, mother* and *friends* at over the 81 percent level but at only 35 percent to the *teacher I fear to be*. *Pupils* were at last admitted to a more intimate group made up of *teacher I would like to be, teacher I am, ideal self, self, parents, friends* and *spouse*.

While many other change-inducing events may have occurred in addition to the FRT, the teachers themselves invariably attributed transformations in their constructs to their enacted roles. As teacher 03 reported, 'the FRT really jolted me to re-examine myself'. The period of enactment was so short that few other major events could have promoted or prevented such change. Another interpretation in such a 'one-group pre-test/post-test' design is that change could have resulted from simple maturation. However, the teachers did not see the differences as arising from the cumulative effects of continued learning. If anything, they felt they had rediscovered the kinds of teachers they had once been. A third rival interpretation concerns the effect of the 'pre-test' itself. Though it may have been possible, if extremely difficult, to present more acceptable versions of the *teacher I am* and of *pupils* in the 'post-test, there was an insistence in the study on there not being any 'right or wrong' points of view. The process of using Repertory grid as an aid to inner conversation was central to the procedure and may legitimately have been a stimulus to confirmation or transformation. The whole purpose of the FRT was to intensify self-consciousness, to heighten sensitivity and perceptiveness, and in some cases to reopen the realms of pedagogic possibility.

When the teachers reflected on the measures of either movement or stability, they agreed in the main that the results closely accorded with their perceptions. As teacher 11 reported:

> The constructs truly reflected my professional concerns at the time of the 'pre-test'; that is, a feeling of impotence and dissatisfaction coupled with an awareness of the need to explore new ways of interpreting my role as a teacher. . . . Something in the mood of my alternative teaching role and the image I had of my new persona stimulated the realisation that my previously unconscious definition of what it meant to be a teacher was unrealistic. This and the sense of liberation that came from being another teacher for ten days are probably the reason for the small measure of similarity (63 per cent) with my post-test. The constructs were more confident in tone and broader in concern. This is consistent with my subjective experience that I was less conscious of experiencing feelings of despair and frustration than at the time of the 'pre-test'.

Before the role enactment, teacher 11 wrote that she was often frustrated by the fact that neither she nor her students lived up to the ideals she had for them all. After the trial period, she stated that her single priority had become to challenge her students – to stimulate them to explore themselves and their world. It seems that teacher 11 had 'got out from under' and was no longer punishing herself for 'failure'. She reported having been touched by her alternative role, particularly by the notion that 'she helps her [students] to assume as much responsibility for their own learning as possible'.

Teacher 12 also found it liberating to recreate her own teaching imaginatively:

> Enacting the role let me see the advantages of an alternative view. I saw that I was now using personal growth as my viewpoint and found teaching . . . a lot more pleasant and satisfying. I felt the children were working . . . with me and not against me as I felt previously. The children . . . were similar to myself and others. Using this perspective I felt better. There was less strain and I performed better.

Teacher 09, whose perspective changed very little, was still able to note:

> I really did feel revitalised – I had let myself slip. I have been struck by the multiplicity of avenues and alternatives that have arisen now within myself. All the training and my abilities have been recalled.

He felt that the FRT gave him the opportunity to explore the long accepted way he had been teaching. However, '. . . several things did not alter much at all. I feel this was largely due to the fact that as a person I already tended to continually review and question my values.'

Those teachers who had been initially very wary or nervous seemed to achieve increased levels of confidence and satisfaction after the FRT. Some other teachers who had been very sceptical experienced many frustrations; however, if their alternative roles had been too easy, the sketches may not have been adequate to lead them to confront personally crucial issues. Such teachers found it difficult to lay aside their usual perspectives and resisted taking themselves in a new way.

One good sign was that most of the teachers found that during the enactment they forgot they were acting. They took over their roles and began improvising freely. Another favourable sign was that successful teachers were often reported as having been perceived by others as having been different. Support reduces threat and helps to produce greater progress. A process of reconstruction had been begun with the teachers feeling that they had genuinely got back in touch with their former teaching selves. As teacher 19 wrote, 'I now have a more relaxed routine that is reminiscent of my former self as a classroom teacher.'

Three teachers were found to be extremely defensive about the FRT and did not seem to want greater clarity as to their actions and the constructs behind them. It may be that people can go out of the theory building business and take advantage of, and even seek, continued ambiguity about their viewpoints. These teachers said they would have preferred to apply Kelly's theory to their students – that would have been more practical. Greene (1988) believes that there are numbed, compliant people to whom it would be cruel to offer the gift of freedom and of self-transformation. Some teachers may prefer peace to freedom of choice. As the Jamesian circus tiger realized, submission to outside forces can bring its own rewards.

A possible danger in FRT is that the teacher educator may appear, like Pablo, as too clever, highly active and manipulative, pushing and prodding, stimulating rather than supporting. I was certainly engrossed in constantly responding to and seeking to meet the 15 teachers' needs. This placed great responsibility on me to avoid giving the impression of being Prometheus-like, bringing fire to those who had eyes but could not see. The aim of the FRT was that the teachers would discover their own fire and open their own doors. The possibility of intrusion was minimized by my being obviously concerned and accessible. The teachers were invited to reflect (and not intimidated into reflecting) upon their own teaching. While most of the teachers found that the FRT gave them the feeling of being in greater control, some still found it a very rational and even a provocative approach, as when unexamined assumptions were challenged during the 'pre-test' mode grid. One of these blind spots concerned whether or not there was a difference in kind between adults and pupils.

FRT is an iconoclastic or transformative venture whereby teachers are placed in new relationships in their classrooms. Reconstruction of perspective is possible when they are able to articulate what concerns them and then to test out the validity of alternative beliefs. The teachers agreed that by the end of the FRT they had been led into a detailed psychological examination of the pedagogy of other approaches to teaching. They often became less centred on their previous teacher viewpoints.

While this study demonstrates a method for promoting perspective trans-formation rather than a substantive pattern, it suggests that FRT can have positive effects when teachers are encouraged to demonstrate their rationality not by commitment to fixed ideas, immutable concepts and stereotyped procedures, but by the way in which, and the occasion on which, they change those ideas, concepts and procedures. In addition, the successful players did not have to be urged to adopt their alternative roles after their enactment because these were automatically accepted if they had been found to be effective. FRT helped to convince the teachers that personal and pedagogical knowledge is constructed and that a wide range of options awaited them. Though they did not all experience the extent of teacher 11's heightened sense of potency and liberation, most at least came to consider whether or not they might devise and then enact their own alternative perspectives.

This chapter has explored a model of in-service teacher education that emphasizes perspectival development and the revising of meaning-making. This is not an easy task – 'to continue be' as Salmon (1988) warned. As against those humanistic writers who portray learning as painless, limitless personal growth, in this kind of approach 'the learning process is often hard and sometimes costly' (Salmon, 1988, p. 12). The Kellyian teaching goal is narrower and more concrete than humanistic self-actualization. The individual's own efforts to reconstrue events effectively form the basis for the development of a new set of personal understandings. The goal of teacher in-service education is not then the distribution of a ready-made package of knowledge, but rather the organization of a personally constructed set of meanings that ramifies within the lives and identities of teachers. The challenge of such experimentation may well prevent the use of control groups that trial nothing new.

Prospect and retrospect is possible only from our own point of view. Each of us looks upon the world of teaching from a particular vantage point that pro-vides a way of interpreting or making sense of events. As Greene (1978, p. 24) wrote, each of us looks upon the common world from 'a particular standpoint, a particular location in space and time. Each of us has a distinctive biography, a singular life history.' And a perspective can always be varied and greater self-consciousness is possible. We cannot but 'future' and think about what might be.

As Sartre (1968) explained, our behaviour is determined not only by our relation to the real, present factors that influence it, but also by a project or certain object, still to come, which it is trying to bring into being. At crucial times, experienced teachers need to stretch their vision and counter the contraction of their cognitive categories. This requires both knowing their own frame of reference and the struggle to get outside of it – or to look at things from another angle. This process is aided by their looking at themselves looking. Any view or construction of teaching is then revealed as correctable and improvable.

Looking back and recapturing their self-delineations and teaching stories may enable teachers to recover their own standpoints on the classroom. By being reminded of the importance of their autobiographical situations and of the ways in which they condition their own perspectives, they may come to understand the provisional nature of all knowing. Making an effort to be mindful and to interpret the texts of their teaching life-stories and by listening to the stories of others who are involved in similar sets of relationships, they may be able to multiply the perspectives through which they look upon the realities of teaching. They may be able to 'choose themselves anew' (Greene, 1978, p. 33) in the light of an expanded interest, of an enriched or transformed sense of reality. By looking from different vantage points they may come to enter new provinces of meaning. Storying or self-narrative procedures enable us to possess greater openness to reawakening and recurring rescue from the ideas and conditions that formed our teaching past.

5

A meeting of perspectives

As shown in Chapter 3, beginning teachers may develop an increasingly negative and apprehensive view of pupils. Zeichner and Tabachnick (1981) and Coulter (1987) indicated that it has become commonly accepted within the teacher education community that pre-service teachers first become more progressive or liberal in their attitudes towards children and education during their periods of university training but that they then shift to the opposing custodial and more traditional view as they move out into their student teaching or practicum and then into in-service experience. The danger is that they may then be passively assimilated into a conservative educational *milieu*. The conceptual shift of attention in teacher education from oneself and subject matter alone to what needs explaining to children is very difficult, especially for beginning teachers. The task is one of thinking not what you know but what they, the pupils, know; that is, not what you find hard but what they find hard. The teachers must learn to put themselves inside their pupils' heads.

This was also the advice of Atticus to his daughter Scout in Harper Lee's (1960) *To Kill a Mockingbird* for getting along with people; that is, that you never really understand them until you consider things from their point of view, until you can climb into their skin and walk around in it. Failure to adopt the perspective of the other may help account for a good deal of misunderstanding. As Kelly (1969) characterized schools, teachers do not understand how their pupils feel, pupils are unable to sympathize with their teachers' frustrations, and teacher educators may not be 'able to put themselves into the shoes' of either.

Teaching is incredibly and unexpectedly demanding and the demands may not be mitigated by skill and experience. In contrast, master chemists may finally produce the desired bubbling green solution in their test tubes, the potential of which is great but the properties of which are mysterious. They sit alone in their laboratory, test tube in hand, brooding about what to do with the bubbling green. Then slowly, however, it dawns on them that it is sitting alone in the test tube brooding about what to do about them! This special nightmare of the chemist is the permanent work-a-day world of the teacher: the bubbling green pupil is always wondering what to do about you, the teacher. If the point of view of pupils in schools is a neglected area in general, then the perceptions that they have of their teachers is a particularly sensitive and even less acknowledged aspect.

'Large as life, and twice as natural': studying student viewpoints

Hunt (1978) argued that, if every person is a psychologist as Kelly hypothesized, then certainly every teacher is a psychologist too. To view teachers as psychologists is to emphasize the importance of their personal conceptions of teaching, that is, their ideas about their goals, their teaching and their students. To accept that teachers are psychologists, however, is to admit that their students are as well, as they also seek to make sense of themselves and their social worlds. Diamond (1983a) explained the writing development of students in terms of the Kellyian view of role. I saw the students' construing of their teachers' personal construct systems as providing a jumping-off ground for the growth of their own perspectives. This learning by transaction was discussed in Chapter 2.

Everything people do, say and even think is a product not only of their personal processes but also of their interaction with other people. People tend to affect the constructions of others in a number of ways: they may change the way reality is seen; they themselves enter into the reality of others; they too have constructions that must be considered in interacting with them; and finally they have their own constructions of the others. The whole notion of the construction of social reality becomes more complex once the possibility is considered that more than one such system exists. Many students' statements, such as 'I think I know what you mean', are indicative of intersubjective or mutual construing in classroom.

Kelly's (1955) commonality corollary states that to the extent that a person uses a construction of experience that is similar to that employed by another, his or her psychological processes are similar to those of the other; that is, as 'birds of a feather', they construe together. Similarity of perspective is fostered by factors such as similarity of role, proximity of location and frequency of interaction. Thus, two classes of year 10 students might have what seem to an observer to be very different teaching–learning experiences and yet they may behave as almost alike, that is, as if they have construed the events in similar ways.

Within a given classroom, commonality alone is still not sufficient for interpersonal understanding or for the process of social interaction. For this the construct system of the other (in this instance, the teacher) has to be subsumed by the pupils. According to Kelly's sociality corollary, to the extent that one person construes the construction processes of another he or she may play a role in a social process involving the other person. This does not imply that there is agreement with the other person's views (for example, 'You mean you want a two page essay for homework?'), but rather that the act of seeking to understand how the other sees things defines a role relationship with them and is linked to behaviour towards them. Contrary to possible charges of fostering privatism, Kelly regards this social aspect of his theory as of central importance. The construing of individuals and groups is negotiated with those with whom they live and work – even with those whom they must respect and obey. Conversely, if teachers do not understand their students, if they do not construe their developing understandings, they may do things to them, but they cannot relate to them.

Teachers and students thus all contribute to the social organization of classroom events, with teaching being a constant process of decision making and trade-off. The teacher and his or her students negotiate and bargain together in order to construct shared classroom meanings, to organize its rules, to live in it as a joint world and to engage in joint actions. However, because of his or her position of power, it is the teacher's constructs that are usually imposed as the defining elements in classroom encounters. To construe their teacher's construction processes so that they can play a social role in classroom processes, the pupils learn to place themselves in the shoes of the teacher and to take the 'attitude of the other'. They are then better able to understand and predict the teacher's present and subsequent behaviour. Interpreting teaching as a joint act does not mean that the protagonists can interact only when they have similar constructs of, for example, written composition. It implies rather that the pupils' construct systems give them a meaningful picture of their teacher's perspectives. The pupils may subsequently wish to help, hinder or remain neutral towards their teachers.

Pupils are particularly alert to the constructions of significant others such as their teachers. To take this view seriously in the way that the social lives of pupils are regarded, means that not only have they inside stories to tell, but also that they are uniquely authoritative, having ownership of their personal domains. Students are not merely the passive recipients of the socializing influences of teachers. They are experts in knowing the sorts of behaviours that are expected of them, as well as the kinds of social negotiation that go on in classrooms. Despite such theoretical acknowledgement, the perspective of pupils is not nearly as well understood as their teachers' and much work still remains to be done. Accordingly, I set about construing pupils' constructions of their teachers in the following way.

Fifteen teachers (5 men and 10 women) from nine large state high schools in south-east Queensland volunteered the co-operation of their year 10 English classes. These teachers represented seven demonstrably salient perspectives on the teaching of composition derived from an original sample of 93 teachers (Diamond, 1979, 1982a). All 15 teachers had received some pre-service teacher education, ranging from 1 to 4 years. Because 11 of the teachers had been teaching in high school for only 1–5 years, they represented a relatively young and inexperienced but recently trained group of specialists. The 15 classes consisted of 372 pupils.

As discussed in previous chapters, the Repertory grid technique remains Kelly's (1955) best known suggestion for eliciting constructs. However, the traditional triadic or 'three-card trick' method of elicitation may be far too complex for children under, say, 12 years or for those who do not have a substantial command of the language of the test. A much wider range of constructs may emerge when students are asked to write short essays, e.g. about children and adults whom they like or dislike. In the present study, the domain to be investigated was pedagogy, that is, the teaching of composition, rather than that of interpersonal relations.

Twenty minutes were allowed for the students' responses. The topic chosen to elicit them was:

> A FRIEND of yours is planning to complete year ten at your school next year. He or she has just written to you asking what they will have to do in order to succeed in WRITING for year ten next year. EXPLAIN how your friend could gain the highest possible grades or marks for writing and also OUTLINE some of the things he or she is likely to ENJOY or find DIFFICULT in being taught how to write.

The student responses were coded by an experienced teacher educator who was otherwise not involved in the study and who aimed to let the categories arise empirically out of the data. First, 178 protocols from 7 of the 15 classes were coded independently by this researcher and myself, with subsequent reconsideration and discussion of responses on which we disagreed. After establishing an acceptable coding procedure, the former analyst coded all the 372 protocols.

The coding first revealed that, while the students made direct statements about how their teachers instructed them, they made many more suggestions about what needed to be done by students in order to succeed. The direct statements were able to be classified into 10 categories, 8 of which had negative as well as positive poles. The bipolar categories were 1, 2, 3, 4, 7, 8, 9 and 10. The components were as follows:

1 *Basic skills*: Parts of speech, clauses and phrases, length, margins, grammar, spelling and punctuation. 'Get it right!'
2 *Teacher's relationship with students*: 'Our teacher is very understanding' *vs*

'They nag a lot' or 'They like to make a fool of you in class'. Supportive or not.

3 *Interest, motivation*: 'They try to make everything as interesting as possible' *vs* 'We don't learn anything' or 'The teacher doesn't make it interesting'.

4 *Workload*: 'It's hard work with a lot of writing' *vs* 'It's easy' with very few restrictions.

5 *Personal development*: 'We are encouraged to write about personal experience' or 'We are free to write as we like'.

6 *Discussion*: Oral work, debates and 'Your own opinion can be given'.

7 *Deductive*: 'We are encouraged to plan our essays and to develop better essays skills' *vs* 'We're not taught about writing essays'.

8 *Topics on set books*: 'The choice is good and interesting' *vs* lack of choice, too artificial and 'The subjects are not good to write about'.

9 *Marking*: 'We're marked for originality and quality rather than quantity' or 'for participation in class' *vs* 'He's a hard marker' or 'There are no helpful comments'.

10 *Time*: 'There's plenty of time' *vs* pressure of insufficient time.

When the complementary suggestions were coded, 12 categories emerged with the following components. Only two of these categories (2 and 11) had negative as well as positive characteristics.

1 *Basic skills*: Neatness, margins, spelling and punctuation.

2 *Teacher–student relationships*: The importance of a good teacher and a sound relationship *vs* the need to 'crawl' to or flatter teachers and to write what they want.

3 *Self-expression*: 'Be honest, write what you think, be natural'.

4 *Student attitudes*: 'Try hard, study a lot, listen to your teacher' and 'Hand your work in on time'.

5 *Growth*: 'Write about your own, personal experiences' and 'Use your imagination'.

6 *Read a lot*: To get knowledge, 'to increase your vocabulary and to see other people's styles'.

7 *Deductive*: 'Plan your work, do rough copies first, capture the reader's attention' and 'Use a mature style'.

8 *Programme organization*: 'Make sure you use time to your best advantage, plan your study' and 'Allow time for revision'.

9 *Transition*: 'Write in your own way but experiment with different techniques' or 'Be descriptive but don't sacrifice narrative qualities' or 'Use your imagination as a mechanical skill'.

10 *Feedback from marking*: 'Learn from your mistakes' *vs* 'Don't let comments upset you' or 'Don't be discouraged by the hard marking'.

11 *Teacher or friend as tutor*: 'See your teacher when you have problems' or 'Get a friend to help you'.

12 *Don't overdo your studies*: 'Don't study too much as it may get you nowhere'.

The 197 direct statements were found to confirm the interpretation of the 1329 suggestions. A total of 89 responses, or 45 percent of the direct statements, related to the basic skills, deductive teaching and to the need to flatter teachers. In order to succeed in composition, students were advised to 'Get it right! Watch parts of speech, clauses, phrases, length, margins, grammar, spelling and punctuation. Plan your essays. Crawl! Become teacher's pet.' When lack of student interest, boring set topics and poor reactions by teachers to student writing are also included, 52 percent of all the direct responses are accounted for.

This negative conclusion is confirmed by another 601 indirect responses, or 45 percent of the student suggestions, which similarly related to the basic skills, deductive teaching and poor teacher–student rapport. If only those clusters of categories that implicate over 75 percent of the total suggestions made about each teacher are considered, 54 percent of the student responses again accentuated the basic skills, deductive teaching and hostile teacher–student contact.

In contrast, when direct statements about not teaching the skills, positive teacher–student relations, interest and teaching for personal growth are examined, they explain only 19 responses or 10 percent of the total. When student suggestions about good teacher–student relations, teaching for growth and self-expression are located, they amount to only 195 responses or 15 percent overall. Of these favourable suggestions, 24 percent referred to only one teacher. Apart from insistence on conscious pre-planning, the single other overwhelming suggestion for success (356 responses or 27 percent) was for students to be positive, to try hard, study a lot, listen to their teachers and to hand in their work on time. This recommended diligence recalls the English morning assembly prayer, 'Teach us, O Lord, to labour and not to ask for any reward, save that of doing Thy will.' One of the main purposes of school may still be to make students work and to keep them busy. If this call to industry is included with the basic skills, deductive teaching and poor interpersonal contact, 72 percent of the responses are explained. While 8 of the 15 teachers could be construed to organize their pedagogical perspective mainly in terms of teaching the mechanical skills, only the one could be characterized in terms of teaching for the development of students' personal resources.

The students thus depicted their experience of being taught composition in the last year of compulsory schooling as fairly bleak. If teachers see themselves as reflected back in the eyes of their students, these derived views are disappointing, even disturbing, and they do not sit easily within the established pedagogical framework. As they become more obvious and pressing, it may come to be recognized that a completely new way of looking at the classroom is needed. Lakatos (1968) described the replacement of one theoretical complex by another with greater explanatory and predictive power as a progressive problem shift. An epistemological breakdown that is followed by a break-through is the typical way a perspective grows and is transformed.

Though there are some exceptions, with teachers 1, 5, 7 and 14 being less formal and beginning to develop a growth-centred model of teaching, the majority of the reported classroom experiences seemed to be surprisingly alike in reflecting the traditional, didactic pedagogy. Despite the cries that continue to go up, the 'basics' model was all but universally put into practice. Though the construct systems of six of the teachers could be described as mixed or transitional, most of the teachers had never abandoned teaching the skills in the classroom. The students quite clearly recognized the perspective featuring the mechanical skills as their teachers' main concern. Many teachers of English may also still be in the forefront of keeping the 'back to basics' movement alive and may even welcome the centralist political perspective discussed in Chapter 1.

The students referred repeatedly to their teachers' insistence on 'good spelling, grammar and punctuation'. The communicated emphasis was clearly on form and the mechanics. Contrary to the clichéd assertion, there was no 'trendy' approach using pop materials. Similarly, neither the Bullock (1975) nor the Kingman (1988) reports could find any evidence of a wholesale move towards informality of teaching methods in British schools. Certainly, these present Australian teachers were not dabbling in permissive, 'soft' or progressive practices either.

So great was the pupils' expressed fear of error-making and subsequent reprisals that they alleged they did not feel free to express themselves. They complained about having to 'stick to one topic', which was often described as 'boring', and also about having to do precisely what was set, even down to completing the exact number of words – a curious carry-over from previous public examinations. The students felt that they were somehow being cheated and even diminished as young people. No matter what they wrote about or how they wrote about it, they believed it would be 'looked down upon'. However, 'you'll do well if you crawl'.

Though some scope was afforded for the imagination, the form of writing that was most prized by the teachers was seen as expository and persuasive. Writing was taught through its transactional mode and was not prepared for by extensive and continuing, personal writing. Worlds of meaning were not being created through writing. The students complained that the formal essay was still the standard by which their writing was judged: 'The thing you might hate in English as I do is writing essays and getting marks for them. . . . The worst thing is having to do essays. . . . All you can do is make certain that your essay is neat and try to make as little [*sic*] mistakes as possible.'

Pupils practise classroom observation every day. While their aims, criteria of significance and contexts of concern are perhaps different from those of a more formal researcher, to a considerable extent the pupils are dependent upon their skill as observers in formulating their next steps in the joint act of the classroom. Together with teacher's practical knowledge or constructs, this natural practice of classroom research by pupils is taken as providing valid evidence as to the ways in which teachers teach. Pupils observe more of the typical behaviour of the teacher than is usually available to an outside observer and, additionally, students are directly participating in the classroom activities.

Underlying the present study there is a set of fundamentally Kellyian notions about the ways in which students relate to their teachers, the classroom and the world. The most important of these is the idea that this relation is active on their part. They do not just sit and wait for the world to impinge upon them. They try to interpret and make sense of it. They grapple with it, they represent it to themselves, they construe it. Donaldson (1978) also depicted children as questioners by nature. They approach the world wondering about it, entertaining hypotheses that they are eager to check – at least when, like Scout, they begin schooling! By directing their questions to other people and to themselves they build up a model of their world, including one of pedagogy. These personal construct systems or inner representations help them to anticipate events and to be ready to deal with them.

In the main, the year 10 students provided a grim definition of their culminating experiences of being taught composition, one that was couched largely in terms of acquiring the basic mechanical skills and of demonstrating obedience. The students themselves felt stigmatized as linguistic vandals. As one student complained:

> Some of the things my teacher wants are just too much, for example, a marchin [*sic*], paragraphs, perfect punctuation, etc. You would have to write in a sentence form and know the adverbs and adjectives etc. You will probably find most of this boring.

Writing came across to the students as rigidly rule-governed and its teaching as often petty and arbitrary.

To transform our perspective on students and to see them, for example, as psychologists, is to remind ourselves of the need to take our students' ideas and intentions into account. For any change to occur, it is necessary that students be construed as like us, their teachers, that is, as constantly engaged in theorizing and experimenting. According to how one person reconstrues others, he or she will moderate his or her own thinking and action in relation to them. Ultimately, education needs to be seen as arising from a specific and personal relationship between teacher and students that can be particularly augmented by writing and sharing (see Chapter 2). Learning then becomes one of the chief means by which young people can develop the capacity to realize themselves as human beings.

When Lewis Carroll's Alice was introduced to the Unicorn as 'large as life, and twice as natural', much like Anne and the little boy whom we met in Chapter 3, it described children as fabulous monsters! Alice quickly retorted that that was how she had felt about mythical unicorns. Together they then made a pact to believe in each other. Perhaps if teachers can believe in students as people they too can be believed in as no less themselves. Nicoll (1989), one of my teacher colleagues, assembled her reflections on seven of her lessons and then contrasted them with those of 24 of her students. She was comforted that many of them seemed to have received 'messages' about education which she believes are representative of her thinking about teaching. Though confronting self can be difficult, Nicoll found that her perspective was widened and her self-awareness sharpened. Mezirow (1981, p. 19) also concluded that through writing or symbolic representation we can dialogue with ourselves and reconstruct the perspective of the other person: 'Perspective taking then becomes an indispensable heuristic for higher level cognitive and personality development.' Becoming conscious of why we attach the meanings we do to reality may be the most significant means to perspective transformation.

Turning on teachers' perspectives

From the above pupil perspectives, some teachers seem to have a very limited appreciation of the learning processes in which their pupils are involved when writing. Perspective transformation represents the most significant kind of learning in teacher education. Both beginning and experienced teachers may need to become more aware of alternative meaning perspectives and to become more open to them. Again, Kellyian procedures can help teachers to spring into a wider meaning world of multiple and moving perspectives and to escape from the constricting ensnarements of traditional one-point, limited perspectives. Teacher education then becomes a matter of travelling with different viewpoints and of escaping being held prisoner of the fixity of any one perspective.

The Repertory grid remains consistent to phenomenology because the method is voluntary, with the person outlining his or her own dimensions for discussion. Unlike behaviouristic approaches to teacher education where the individual merely responds to the environment as when drilled in microteaching, the teacher when viewed as a personal scientist has the capacity to represent and thereby interpret, construe and reconstrue his or her classroom. The Repertory grid produces unique semi-autobiographical accounts of how the world of teaching is anticipated and how its players and plot are evaluated (see Chapters 3 and 4). However, before considering what the other – the pupil – is like, teachers may first need to consider things from their own point of view. They may need to enter into their own phenomenal worlds more deeply, to explore where they are looking from and to 'square' themselves with themselves. Teachers may then need to be willing to open their minds to possibilities contrary to what has been regarded previously as perfectly obvious.

Clinical or case study evidence helps to reverse the contraction of teachers' perspectives and is itself characterized by a human immediacy and inter-subjectivity that transcends formulations derived from behaviouristic patterns of thought. Teacher educators can make their own perceptions and thoughts more reliable in the face of teachers' verbal and social expressions by putting subjectivity into the centre of the inquiry. There is an inescapable core of disciplined subjectivity and sociality which it is neither possible nor desirable to replace with seemingly more 'objective' methods. Instead, teacher educators can invite their teachers to look at themselves with the help of more explicit theories and techniques. They can proceed collaboratively with a systematic orientation based on a more coherent world image. A 'free-floating' or open attention waits to be impressed by the teachers' recurring themes and then to find the zone for particular exploration. Helping teachers find better ways to teach is indeed shared research in progress.

A clinical method

After Kelly (1955) construed people generatively as inquirers, and pre-emptively as nothing but bundles of constructs (that is, as the intersect of many personal construct axes), he devised the Repertory grid for eliciting and then comparing and contrasting their differing mind-space structures. Kelly (1955, p. 299) considered it appropriate to factor analyse grids in terms of 'factorial figures' as well as in terms of 'factorial constructs'. The identity of the factorial figure (such as *self*, the *teacher I am*, the *teacher I would like to be*, the *teacher I fear to be* and *pupils*) is expressed in terms of a derived set of ratings that constitutes a mathematical statement. The figure finds its place in terms of many dimensions of consideration to develop psychological character and uniqueness.

In order to place themselves in a position to play a role in helping teachers, teacher educators and researchers may need to understand how the teachers, like their pupils, build their own matrices of approval. Because the Repertory grid provides a mathematical basis for expressing and measuring the per-ceptual relationships between the role elements or figures that are character-istically interwoven in any person's meaning space, Kelly sought a simple way of factoring such space. However, while it is one thing to articulate teachers' personal construct systems in this way, it is quite another for teacher educators then to subsume them within their own systems in ways that enable them to deal effectively with their teacher-learners. As Kelly (1955, p. 277) asked:

> Can we, as rank outsiders, crawl into this subject's skin and peep out at the world through his eyes? Perhaps not. But it should be possible to derive data from his protocol which can be meaningfully perceived within our own personal construct systems.

Some advice about the interpretation of pedagogical grids is offered below by making some basic and practical points about how to help teachers become more aware of their tacit understandings and perspectives and how to explore what they involve. This requires that teacher educators enter into teachers' perspectives together with them. Other accounts relevant to this collegial role are provided by Thomas (1979), Shaw (1980) and by Pope (1978). The aim is to make questionable the categories or constructs that have contained teachers' lives. The first step is to 'unconceal' (Greene, 1988, p. 58), to create clearings, spaces in the midst of which new teacher decisions can be made. It is to break through the masked and the falsified, to reach toward what is half-hidden or concealed. If the world of the classroom refers to interpreted experience, it might indeed 'split open' if we all learn to listen and to pay heed.

Exploration of teachers' constructs: the FOCUS technique

If, as the organization corollary suggests, teachers' perspectives are not just chaotic jumbles but rather related, hierarchical and integrated complexes, these networks of pathways may be regarded as being more or less similar and their equivalence or functional overlap (and also that of elements) can be determined. While primarily psychological in nature, this degree of similarity was expressed by Kelly in a coefficient of similarity that resembled the old simple matching coefficient.

Several other relational measures have since been introduced for discovering the principles of inclusiveness which underlie groupings. While the Pearson product–moment correlation coefficient is most familiar and widely used, Minkowski's city block metric is a mathematically more sophisticated distance measure of similarity with respect to the construct of matching (see Shaw, 1980). This metric provides a cumulative distance score. For constructs, the coefficient is an association or similarity measure and it ranges from -100 (for maximum or perfectly reversed similarity) through 0 (for complete dissimilarity) to $+100$ percent (for maximum or perfect similarity). For elements, the coefficient is a distance measure that ranges from 0 (for maximum distance) to 100 percent (for mimimum distance or perfect similarity). The matching scores are used in the FOCUS algorithm to generate matrices of dis/similarities between constructs and elements, respectively, which are then used to form clusters.

The FOCUS technique also provides criteria for reversing a construct if it is better matched in its reversed than in its actual form. Kelly (1955) used a process of reflection or reversal in analysing grids and this operation is important because the assignment of left-hand or emergent and right-hand or implicit poles to a construct is clearly artificial. Unless some additional rationale is operating, these poles may be revised providing the assignment of the elements to the poles is also reversed.

One of the most appealing features of FOCUS is that, as a two-way cluster analysis, it sorts the constructs and the elements into linear sets so that the constructs closest together in the space are also closest together in the order, as also are the elements. An advantage of the presentation is that the sorting only re-presents the original grid organized by the 'neighbourness' of constructs and elements. The main structure and patterns are identified and there is nothing mystical in the way that the parts of the grid are rearranged. The analysis process can be easily understood by both the generator and the user of the grid. The teachers project meaning onto the results, which they confirm directly in term of their original grids with the help of the teacher educator.

The SOCIOGRIDS technique

This technique was developed by Thomas *et al*. (1976) to map one grid onto another so that either grids elicited from the same teacher (or from a group) over a period of time can be compared and contrasted or the constructions among a group of teachers can be explored. Independently of the words used to label constructs, the PAIRS algorithm computes the measure of operational similarity or overlap between each two grids. This matrix of similarity measures serves as the basis for generating a sociometric type of display showing who construes what most like whom. All the constructs from all the grids are then listed to produce a continuum ranging from those that are most shared by the group to those that are least common. A mode grid or shared perspective is extracted from the mode constructs, which usually consist of the same number as elicited in each of the individual grids.

While there may be reservations about the legitimacy of grouping such diverse perceptions into a common view, Kelly (1955, p. 318) hoped that some methodology would prevent grids from becoming 'bogged down' in a particularistic approach. If the elements are comparable from protocol to protocol, it is possible to extract a group stereotype or factorialized figure such as, for example, of *self*, the *teacher I am* and *pupils*. As the commonality corollary assumes, areas of shared or continuing meaning between and within individuals are essential and usual.

A workshop interpretation

Although Kelly discussed the characteristics that make for greater flexibility in construct systems, more attention still needs to be paid to specific ways in which the development of perspectives can be effectively helped or hindered. Carefully guided talkback through the patterns of meaning latent within the display of the original raw grids can help teachers as star- or cluster-gazers to interpret the meanings in significant and personally relevant terms.

A workshop in several steps was designed as an adaptation of Shaw's (1980) procedures to take teachers back through their individual and shared grids. As discussed in Chapters 3 and 4, the grids were completed by 17 beginning teachers during a year-long course of teacher preparation (Diamond, 1985a) and by 15 experienced teachers before and after individually designed interventions in the form of Kelly's fixed role treatment (Diamond, 1985b). As a conversational heuristic, the focused grids proved a useful, speculative tool, which reflected back to the teachers their views of themselves and teaching as seen through their own eyes and even as in process of transformation.

As detailed below, steps 1–11 helped in talking about each grid and steps 13–15 in discussing a sequence of two or three grids. The shared list of elements consisted of 16 figures for the beginning teachers and of 15 for the experienced teachers (see Tables 1 and 5). Twelve constructs were elicited from each teacher on each occasion using the same figures, i.e. *self, past self, ideal self, teacher I am, teacher I would like to be, teacher I fear to be, mother, father, siblings, spouse/steady, friends, pupils, principal/deputy, subject master, supervising teacher/inspector* and *university tutor* (if applicable). The effects of the practicum experiences and of enacting the alternative scenarios were monitored by steps 16–18. The workshop thus attempted to focus and discipline the teacher educator's awareness by attention being devoted first to the exploration and then to the elaboration of the teachers' constructs.

Interpreting a cluster analysis of your Repertory grids on people and teaching

Grid 1: FOCUS

1 Write briefly about your reaction to doing the grid. How did you feel? What were you thinking about?

2 Does your list of bipolar constructs seem personally valid? How well does it represent your ideas and concepts?

3 Are any constructs reversed in the focused, reordered version of your raw grid? They will be listed after the matrix of construct matching scores and before your construct tree diagram.

4 By examining their verbal labels can you detect any one or two major themes running through your constructs? What are these super-ordinates or unifying threads? Is there a central metaphor that encapsulates your view of people and teaching? What tone or feeling emanates from it?

5 From the upper and lower triangular matrices of construct matching scores find, say, two pairs of constructs with the highest percentage of match. The scores will range from −100 percent for perfect but reversed similarity through 0 percent for complete dissimilarity to +100 percent for maximum similarity. Find one pair of constructs with the lowest score. What are they? Do these relationships make sense to you?

6 From the upper right half matrix of element matching scores, find,

say, two pairs of elements with the highest percentage of match. Find one pair with the lowest. What are they? Do these relationships make sense to you?

7 Still looking at the element matrix, which elements were most highly related to elements 4, 5, 6 and 12 (the *teacher I am*, the *teacher I fear to be*, the *teacher I would like to be*, and *pupils*)? Which one is least related to them? How were the four elements interrelated with one another?

8 Draw your FOCUS-ed grid's element and construct trees:
   (i)   Which constructs are to reversed (see 3 above)? Print the emergent poles to the left hand of the grid and the implicit poles to the right hand.
   (ii) Cut out your construct tree and attach it to the right hand of the grid ensuring that the constructs are correctly aligned.
   (iii) Draw your construct tree by following the appropriate instructions.
         If there are 12 constructs, your first cluster will be 13. Continue sequentially.
   (iv) Draw your element tree by following the appropriate instructions.
         If there are 15 elements, your first cluster will be 16. Continue sequentially.

9 *Construct clusters.* Looking at the percentage of match or similarity (100–30 percent) at the top of your construct tree, are there 2 or 3 construct clusters at, say, better than 70 percent match? Separate these constellations by broken lines. Looking at each cluster, which constructs are most highly associated? These highly related constructs give identity to each of your clusters. Print these clusters as a list of superordinates.

10 *Element clusters.* Proceed as for the constructs in 9 above except that the percentage of match ascends the left-hand margin. In what family or group have you located the *teacher I am*, the *teacher I fear to be*, the *teacher I would like to be* and *pupils*?

11 *Central characterizations.* Look down column 4 to find how you have delineated for yourself the *teacher I am*. Using the ratings assigned (1 = extremely whatever the emergent pole is; 2 = the emergent pole; 3 = undecided; 4 = the implicit pole; and 5 = extremely whatever the implicit pole is) to this element on each of the 12 constructs, write out your self-description of the *teacher I am*. Repeat the procedure for the *teacher I fear to be*, and *teacher I would like to be* and *pupils* (elements 5, 6, and 12).

Grid 2: FOCUS

12 Repeat steps 1–11 as above.

Comparing grids 1 and 2 pre- and post-intervention: SOCIOGRIDS

13 Grids 1 and 2 are compared by means of a percentage in the gridmix matrix of similarity measures. What is the percentage of match between your two grids, that is, between the 'pre-' and 'post-tests'? Has your construing changed very much? A figure of 80 percent may suggest a degree of continuity, 60 percent a deal of change, while a smaller figure may represent substantial transformation of perspective.

14 Look at the upper right triangular matrix (24 × 24) of construct matching scores. Draw a diagonal from the score in row 1 under column 13 to the scores in row 12 under column 24 (see Pope, 1978). These 12 percentages show the different matching scores or degrees of similarity obtained for each construct with itself so that the first number (row 1, column 13) indicates the degree of match for construct 1 between the two occasions. If it is low, then the construct has changed; if high, it has not. Find the constructs which have changed most from the pre- to the post-test and then those which have remained the same.

15 *Complete the following:*
    (i) 'I changed my mind about. . . . This was because. . . .'
    (ii) 'I did not change my mind about. . . . This was because. . . .'

16 *Transformation or continuity.*
    (i) What changes have taken place in your construct and element clusters (see 9 and 10 above)?
    (ii) Compare your 'pre-' and 'post-test' delineations of: the *teacher I am*, the *teacher I fear to be*, the *teacher I would like to be* and *pupils*.
    (iii) Have the gaps between these elements remained the same, widened or narrowed after the intervention (fixed role treatment)? What do your verbal descriptions (11 above) of these four elements on the two occasions reveal?

17 Did any event or feature of the intervention (the year of pre-service education or your alternative role sketch) contribute either to movement or to resistance to change? Is the second state one of rigidity or of stability?

18 Comment on Kelly's (1969, p. 64) view:
    The FRT [or practice teaching] is not a panacea but an experiment. The important thing is not that it gives the [teacher] an authentic way to [teach] but that it invites him [or her] to try a new way, calculated and venturesome and to appreciate its outcomes. . . . The only valid way to [teach] is to get on with it.

Exploration of teachers' constructs

Though the elicitation process itself may trigger off reflexive mechanisms, careful talkback can further enhance the teachers' awareness of their own construing; that is, if good questions are asked rather than pat answers being found. Salmon (1978, p. 36) has described such questions as those which 'avoid confusion and transcend the obvious or the trivial'. A renewal in teaching perspective may begin by construing *self* and the *teacher I am* with a view to producing something new rather than by preoccupying itself with discrediting prior constructions. Teaching is then regarded,

> as open to an infinite variety of alternative constructs – some of them better than others, to be sure – and with most of the best ones yet to be concocted. In such a system the function of an answer is not to make further questioning unnecessary but to hold things together until a round of better questions has been thought up.
>
> (Kelly, 1969, p. 116)

Easterby-Smith (1980) warns, however, that the potential for quantification can lead to an overemphasis on the numbers in the grid and these can exert something of a mesmeric effect upon the teacher educator. Indeed, Neimeyer (1985) has shown that, while over 95 percent of published empirical studies in personal construct theory employ some variant of the grid, serious studies of the evolution or flow of perspectives or of conceptual structures are rare.

If they use the grid, teacher educators and researchers may need to remember that a construct or a cluster of constructs is a psychological process of a live teacher. It is not,

> an intangible essence that floats from the owner to the interpreter of the grid on the wings of an uttered word. While [teacher educators] can fill the air with words that symbolise their own notions, they must avoid confusing the [teachers] by helping them to develop new constructs out of the materials they are able to furnish.
>
> (Kelly, 1955, p. 1088)

The words passing between them need to be valued in terms of what they mean to the teachers and not because of the alleged natural correctness of the teacher educators' interpretations. All the interpretations that are understood by teachers are perceived in terms of their own construct systems. The teachers can be asked to conceptualize in some new or generalized form what they have been talking about only if it is stressed that not only is a construct 'personal' but also that it is a 'process' that goes on inside a person and that it always expresses anticipation. When this is forgotten, the clusters are reduced to static, geographic concentrations of ideas. However, if pupils have been construed as stupid and yet calculating, and teachers as wise and cruel, that is something to prompt action in tomorrow's classroom.

Teachers' clustering or association of constructs and elements provides one of the best bets to surfacing the meaning of teaching as teachers currently conceive of it. By discussing such constellations, teachers may be helped to become more 'considerate' of their own perspectives (see Barthes, 1977). There is a synthesizing function that can be assumed to associate, cluster or condense such items into strong images and affects, mostly without conscious knowledge. Teacher educators and researchers can rely on the teachers' capacity to produce such sequences of themes, thoughts and affects which then seek their own concordance and provide their own cross-references. This synthesizing trend permits teacher educators to observe with the 'free-floating attention' mentioned above and to expect a confluence of the teachers' search for clarification and their own endeavour to subsume meaning and relevance. Kelly (1969) advised that the need at this time is to stop wondering what the words literally mean. Try to recall, instead, what they sound like. 'Disregard content for the moment; attend to theme' (Kelly, 1969, p. 229).

Care needs to be taken that teachers continue to play a major part in interpreting the grid and that the computer printout does not form a barrier to their understanding and action. Focusing adds nothing new to a grid but only makes it easier to identify the hidden patterns. While summarizing and condensing the data, Kelly (1969, p. 290) insisted that:

> neither abstraction nor generalization has ever been computerised. . . . What can be . . . is the elimination of redundancy in a construction matrix. The resultant shrinkage . . . is sometimes mistaken for abstraction. . . . But the contribution the computer makes is to economy of the language employed, not to conceptualization.

The FOCUS-ed grid provides an economical, spatial representation of how teachers classify teaching and these perspectives can be extended and even transformed by asking further questions around the grid. As the teachers seek to enter their own (and even group) construing, some personally significant perceptual, cognitive and affective organizations or schemata may be challenged as new perspectives on familiar figures emerge and the teachers find themselves thinking, feeling and perceiving differently.

Elaboration of teachers' constructs

Kelly's most distinctive theme is his concern not only with the exploration of systems of personal understandings but also with their elaboration and revision. If there is no test of their validity, there is little point in the most detailed and careful inquiry into teachers' theories of the classroom. The mere identification of their ways of knowing does not guarantee their validity. Once explicated, their meanings require further experimentation and validation. A focus on, and an evaluation of, the teachers' central assumptions requires that the teacher educators act as tentative 'process consultants' who can promote movement through the creativity cycle.

Individual sessions with members of the two groups of teachers outlined above, and especially with the more experienced group, were based on the individual FOCUS-ed grids, the mode grids and socionets, the construct and the element trees, the self-delineations of the centrally important elements (such as the *teacher I am* and *pupils*) and the distance scores for these selected elements. As closing or widening gaps between elements were hit upon, this often had the effect of 'a crystal seed in a supersaturated solution: a rush of other insights and explanations quickly formed around it' (Tiberius, 1980, p. 6). The seed acted as a kernel of truth in the limited hermeneutic sense of truth as an interpretive view of things, rather than as a 'once and for all time', settled view of the 'true' state of affairs.

As puzzling relationships seemed to fall into place, the teachers often showed surprise quickly followed by recognition. There ensued a natural process of building, shaping and clarifying, which yielded information sufficiently detailed to be useful in helping the teachers to construe their ongoing or slowing processes of transformation. It was possible for them to grasp the details of a particular issue, such as their inability to realize personal teaching ideals or to deal with their alienation from pupils, and then to co-design a course of action (such as enactment of an alternative teaching scenario) to effect possible improvement or resolution. As step 11 showed above, the ratings assigned on each of the constructs to key elements such as the *teacher I am*, the *teacher I would like to be* and *pupils* helped to regulate the design of such fixed role treatments.

The process of perspective transformation was enhanced by the experience of mutual stimulation which generated a more narrowly specific and deeper appreciation of their own teaching circumstances. The initial analytical or exploratory stage was thus followed by a productive or synthetic phase of elaboration so that the set of personally significant issues suggested by the grids was followed by a behaviour experiment. While a large number of potentially useful resources and recommendations might have been offered, I made specific suggestions in the form of questions to help launch the teachers farther into their own voyages of self-discovery. Often, by acting not as a detached expert but rather as a facilitator, mediator, co-problem-solver and advocate, I found that successful recommendations were developed cooperatively.

Shifts in perspective can be indicated by changes in distance. The matrices of element matching scores, described by Easterby-Smith (1980, p. 21) as 'standard scores for the grid', thus proved to be a particularly rich source of prompting questions and these, when embodied as fixed role treatments, helped the further transformation over time of the teachers' perspectives. The distance between the *teacher I am* and *self* was initially construed as an index of role identification; that between the *teacher I am* and the *teacher I would like to be* as a measure of self-esteem or of realization of positive teaching ideals; that between the *teacher I am* and the *teacher I fear to be* as a sign of escaping from a negative pedagogic self-image; and that between the *teacher I am* and *pupils* as a measure of empathy for or alienation from them. However, it is essential to establish the behavioural significance and the interpretations of the teachers themselves of such shifts and to keep clear the rationale for their construction. For example, increasing distance between *self* and the *teacher I am* might not automatically indicate a lack of dedication to teaching as a career but rather a conscious decision by an individual to have a personal life quite independent of his or her professional calling.

The goal of a method of teacher education that seeks to promote the development of perspectives is to help teachers understand and either remedy problems or confirm solutions in their classroom teaching and learning. Such a method is distinguished from more narrowly scientific modes by the intensive study of individual teachers, by the use of repeated grid measures in conjunction with collaboratively designed interventions and by role changes consonant with more collegial relations among the participants. The FOCUS technique can be used to examine the changing constructions of teachers. The extension of FOCUS to multiple constructions of the same elements through the program SOCIOGRIDS is a useful tool for tracking changes in the structure of individual and shared perspectives.

Cluster analysis is a distance-based means of analysis that provides a method of clustering constructs and elements in such a way that feedback is provided on possible structures underlying the construction processes. Through the structure that is displayed is limited in its semantics to a symmetric relation of neighbourness between the clustered items, conversations with teachers suggest that wider interpretations may also be possible. Cluster analysis is essentially exploratory in nature and probably has its principle usefulness at the frontier of inquiry in teaching education where basic and fruitful concepts are rare. As a method, it has the important role of enabling the drawing of a first crude map of a perspective subsequently to be re-surveyed by its owner.

Although a multivariate statistical procedure, cluster analysis differs from the 'established approach' (Lunt and Livingstone, 1989, p. 530) to statistical inference because it maximizes validity by revealing latent order or structure within data to permit more varied and complex conceptualizations of structure. Cluster analysis does not attempt to reduce data to a single point. Any generalization to wider populations remains an issue of interpretation and of taking questions of pedagogy and psychology into account. FOCUS and SOCIOGRIDS allow for the explanation of teachers' theories that are not easily fitted into the logic of the null hypothesis.

Cluster analysis produces results about distances, connections and relationships, which can be expressed through Kelly's basic notions of similarity and matching. A conversational workshop approach can help teacher educators to talk teachers back through their FOCUS-ed grids so that together they can learn to experience teaching as a current enterprise and not merely as an accomplished fact. While the teacher educator uses the grids as the basis of the conversation, the teachers increasingly take responsibility for the content and meaning of the exchange.

Exploring and elaborating teachers' construct systems confirms that teaching is about making sense of things and that the sense that is achieved is not some generalized, abstract or disembodied knowledge. It is understanding framed within personal contexts, constraints, opportunities and time-scales (Salmon, 1978). Finally, the central feature of it all, despite the generalizations of the mode grids, is the absence of any one final vision of teaching.

If teachers can see themselves as exploring only one of many possible perspectives on teaching, with some of the best yet to be devised, they can be on the lookout for fresh viewpoints emerging out of their experiences of teaching. As Kelly (1969) advised, a voyage upon which no person has ever embarked produces no landfalls, but one which people have pursued to its mysterious destination may then be left in order to launch a wiser venture. 'Ships are built to be sailed. Ideas are meant to be enacted rather than preserved. The truths we seek . . . [to] pattern our search are as transient as they are vital to the success of the human venture' (Kelly, 1969, pp. 138–9).

Teacher education may be usefully construed as helping teachers to 'turn on' the navigation lights of their own construct systems. Clinical-based evidence helps them to interrogate their own points of view. Explanation at the individual level occurs through such processes as searching for the individual's understandings and looking for the idiographic patterns within them. By organizing all the information, the teacher's perspective becomes more intelligible and capable of revision. While the analyses in the preceding chapters may seem to produce a tangle of details, including percentages and clusters, it is exactly such details that are essential to reconsidering a teacher's perspective. The Kellyian approach focuses on a micro-anatomy consisting of the teacher's recurring constructs or bipolar opposites. These units are taken as providing the key to perspectival functioning.

A major theme of both teacher and pupil accounts of school appears to be a feeling of isolation and exclusion, a feeling that formal education offers little scope for personal choice or individual initiative. In the next two chapters, further means of safeguarding and of elaborating their subjective points of view are explored. While each person seeks to communicate in the terms that make sense to them, this may not necessarily be in terms that make the same sense to others. Growth for teachers may consist in their learning to problematize their own practice and to pose their own teaching dilemmas.

6

Ways of eliciting teachers' self-narratives

Teachers' perspectives or outlooks cannot be transformed nor newly attained unless there is some comprehensive overview within which they can first be construed. The emergent perspectives that teachers gain need to be construed by them if any sense is to be made out of them. Two main ways of encouraging the reconstruction of teacher perspective through obtaining a metaperspective were trialled in the previous chapters. In the first, teachers are helped to reconsider how they cluster their teacher selves and pupils and then the reasons for their superordinate structures are creatively sought out. In the second, a detailed fixed-role teaching sketch is collaboratively drafted and then creatively enacted. Both sets of approaches use Kelly's (1955) creativity cycle so that, while teachers may begin by loosely construing their teacher components and teaching roles, they quickly move into the tightening phase of validation by seeking to translate the fresh insights and the alternative scenarios into their daily teaching. Reconstruction of perspective is aided by the release and harnessing of their pedagogic imagination.

Storying is the subject of the final two chapters and provides a third approach to reconstruction by writing and reading, by composing and responding. The advantage of creative activity is not 'busy-ness' for its own sake nor play for release. Rather it is a form of experimentation involving the design, execution and genuine appraisal of outcomes against anticipations. The task for teacher education is to assist teachers in maximizing the experimental characteristics of their teaching ventures. The aim is promote not just the efficiency and effectiveness of systems but the continuous formation of individual teacher selves through speculative audacity, choice of action and creative productions.

A science of stories

The giving and taking of stories, or the science of stories, is crucial not only for teacher education but also for educational research. Answers to questions posed by Gregory (1966) below reveal something of the significant differences between traditional transmissive and psychometric approaches in education and psychology and those that are more critical and interpretive. As in Chapter 5, he asked: 'When did you last hear of laboratory bound scientists talking to the experimental material in their test tubes and when did you hear of its talking back to them?' They do not ask questions of it and it certainly asks none of them! In contrast, the objects, or more properly the subjects, of inquiry in educational research are, like the researchers themselves, human beings and education is potentially and even distinctively rich in opportunities for dialogue. Even 'experimental' has often come to mean rigidly rule-governed and methodologically precise rather than exploratory and innovative. The reproduction of knowledge has been prized over its generation and the social sciences have been seen as natural rather than human sciences. But not universally.

White (1975) intensively studied three lives in progress. The individuals were studied first when they were college students, then 5–10 years later and subsequently past their fiftieth birthdays. Central to the study was White's belief that as a living organism, a person is to some degree a centre of force capable of having effects on the environment. Much as we are moulded by circumstances, it is not entirely beyond us to do some moulding of our own. 'Human behaviour exhibits qualities of selecting, construing, testing, organizing and persisting, all of which tend to produce movement toward bettering one's personal situation' (White, 1975, p. 2). Individual activity and initiative have been too often neglected by education and science. The extent of this bias against individuality, multiplicity and continuous change can be appreciated by contrasting the scientific approach with that of the biographer or novelist. While growth and transformation is a prominent theme in such literary approaches, scientific approaches seek the fixed, the repetitive and the unspontaneous in human life and ignore the changing, the designing, the farsighted and the creative.

In contrast, Sacks (1985) felt compelled to speak of tales and fables, as well as of singular cases, and remembered that Luria liked to speak of a personalistic or 'romantic science' as the intersection of fact and fable. To restore the human subject at the centre, even case histories must be deepened to a 'faction' and the essential feeling of a life must be preserved. The mental processes that constitute our being and life are not merely abstract and mechanical but personal as well. These processes involve not just classifying and categorizing but also constant judging and feeling. The danger is that 'a science which eschews the judgemental, the particular, the personal . . . becomes entirely abstract and computational' (Sacks, 1985, p. 19). The concrete in contrast is readily imbued with feeling and meaning so that it moves easily into the symbolic. Too often, however, by a process of vertical reductionism, the abstract has been separated from the phenomena themselves.

If our behaviour is largely controlled by our interpretation of events and if reality is constituted by our internal fictions, language and its productions can give us the most immediate access to them. Storying or our instinct for fabulation needs then to be taken seriously and appreciated. Our essential task as learners, teachers, educators and researchers, and we all are all of these, is to be storytellers with what Mair (1987, p. 3) described as 'a profound concern for what is involved in the stories that we live and the stories that we tell'. Stories are constitutive of ourselves as they embody and direct our thoughtscapes and personal histories. While we all struggle to make sense of our lives and our occupations in the course of experiencing ourselves and our relationships with others, each of our lives is itself a personal and unreplicable experiment of self, a unique tale or narrative.

Just as the novelist Henry James understood the world and the stream or channel of consciousness differently from his psychologist brother, William James, the storying or narrative way of human knowing may be seen as textual rather than logical. Unlike the way that propositional or conceptual knowing consists of explanations and cause and effect, the narrative or symbolic mode of making sense provides the natural means of depicting human predicaments such as inhere in becoming and remaining a teacher. Realizing that teaching is not just telling, that learning is not just listening and that learning how to learn is not just submitting to being taught, may represent transformations of understandings. By unpacking these presuppositions as revealed in our narratives, we can escape from our own implicitness and scrutinize our present point of view. Each of us uses a particular peephole through which we scan the world for the blips of meaning and the sequences that we construct.

Narrative can be considered as a basic metaphor for understanding human experience and behaviour. Narrative is such a daily and universal activity that Hardy (1987) described it as our primary act of mind. Because we all create our own sustained mind fictions, narrative is not just an aesthetic invention used only by artists to control, manipulate and order events in books. Everyone makes up stories about themselves and others in order to live. By constructing our narratives we make sense of our world and our place in it. However, by considering what was and what might be we are then better able to change what is. Through self-narratives we can devise and consider other alternative, possible realities. If we are to control and direct our own thinking and teaching lives, both of which are fictive processes, we must begin by becoming more conscious of them.

Writing is first a complex form of consciousness and then also a means of heightening it. But what is organized in our narratives then is far more than words. As Bruner (1986, 1987) has shown, we construct ourselves autobiographically because there is no other way of describing experience or lived time. A life is a narrative achievement and recounting it as an interpretive feat.

Our narratives allow us to reflect on our experience and in so doing we can sort out, make sense of and come to terms with ourselves and our world. In Britton's (1970) description of the endless process, we construct a representation of the world as we experience it, and from this representation, or cumulative record of our past, we generate expectations concerning the future which, as moment by moment, the future becomes the present, enable us to interpret the present. These personally forged anticipations are revealed in our narratives and by attending to them we can take greater responsibility and direct our teaching lives. The challenge for teacher education is to facilitate as full a subjective view as possible and to promote its sensitive transformation.

To change our stories is to change our lives. Each of us lives, learns and teaches a story that represents ourselves alone and, though we do not entirely govern what happens to us, we create what we make of what does happen. We each construct the meaning of our story, which gives our lives 'their essential shape, defines their heights, their plateaux, their declines, marks out their movement, direction, changes in direction' (Salmon, 1985, p. 138). In teaching, we tell our own stories. As the authors of our personal story, we select what belongs to the story and what lies outside. As authors, we have agency. The main character in each of our individual stories is the self and it is more than a haphazard collection of autobiographical data. Self is what we believe ourselves to be, the story of us that we tell ourselves. It is the superordinate or core meaning that we attach to our lives.

Our growth as teachers may consist in turning around on our sense of teacher self and then remaking it. Our Repertory grid self-delineations and our self-narratives can both reveal and help cure 'our certain blindness'. As William James (1913) explained, while the whole truth is not revealed to a single observer, each of us gains a partial insight from the peculiar position in which we stand. Our accounts of our teaching lives reveal our actions as human agents and as participants in social life. By showing what is and by entertaining possible alternatives, the writing and the reading of narrative helps alter what we do. We need to learn that the world of our present consciousness is only one out of many worlds that exist, and that those other worlds must contain experiences that have a meaning for our life also.

Prompts to self-narrative

Thomson (1985) described how the Longsearch group of teachers to which he belonged met regularly to share and examine their experiences of classroom practice by way of in-service education. They tried a number of 'mirrors', including video- and cassette-recording, the Flanders Interaction Analysis Categories (FIAC), triangulation, transcriptions and diaries or journals. The much used video-recording of teaching was found to be disappointing in practice because of the difficulties entailed in having the equipment at hand, setting it up and overcoming technical and operational problems. The technical reality of what ended up on tape was their greatest disappointment, from the unselective recording of every sound to coping with the restricted picture resolution. The Flanders category system also required outside assistance and was not felt to be appropriate, even when modified to meet their particular teaching needs. While classroom visitors may help triangulate the perceptions of the teacher and the pupils, some third persons unfortunately construed themselves as authority figures rather than as equal partners in the enterprise.

In contrast, transcription of the audio-recorded material was found to be invaluable. However laborious the continuous review to ensure its accuracy, transcription served to sharpen the teachers' perceptions of the classroom experience. They found that any form of written documentation on classroom events was the most useful of the mirrors they used. Recollections entered in journal form or a daily diary were found to provide the most revealing insights into the continuities of teaching. The equipment this entailed was minimal, the records could be searched quickly, summarized as needed and easily reproduced. While it may not be convenient and indeed impossible to get at our teaching minds through narrowly empirical or psychometric means which, at their most psycho-physical, may be described as 'the ear-nose-and-throat' approach, our detailed teaching perspectives can be easily yielded by using storying procedures such as discussed below. The suggestions that follow are illustrative rather than exhaustive and are intended to stimulate the invention of even more ways of arousing aspects of our submerged consciousness.

Autobiography

Kelly (1969) used an autobiographical essay to recall his life between taking first-year psychology and receiving his PhD. He taught soap-box oratory in a labour college of labour organizers, government in an Americanization institute for prospective citizens, public speaking for the American Bankers Association, and 'dramatics in a junior college' (Kelly, 1969, p. 48). He had taken a master's degree by studying workers' use of leisure time and an advanced education degree at Edinburgh. He had also dabbled academically in education, sociology, economics, labour elections, biometrics, speech pathology and cultural anthropology and had majored in psychology for a grand total of 9 months in 1930. In addition to this time-line, he provided an intellectual autobiography of his own theory and of his initiation of his own actions:

> I feel myself uniquely qualified to write this account because I wrote the theory also, though I realise that writing a theory does not necessarily mean you know how you came by it. . . . I can at least write about what I now recall.
>
> (Kelly, 1969, p. 46)

Elvin's (1987) educational autobiography, *Encounters with Education*, provided an account of the life of an educator which is valuable not only to its author but which is relevant also to the concerns that are still very much part of any teaching life. The first half of the account, called 'Getting an education', dealt with Elvin's early home life, the experience of primary school in the early years of this century, his life as a scholarship holder at high school in Essex, then as an undergraduate at Cambridge in the 1920s and as a visitor at Yale. In the second half, 'Providing an education', he described his life in education as a don in the 1930s, as Principal of Ruskin College, Oxford, then Director of the UNESCO Education Department and, finally, as Director of the University of London Institute of Education. What Elvin particularly communicated was his own sense of the importance of education.

From Augustine, Tolstoy, Sartre, Popper, Churchill, Merton, and Bertrand Russell to Bruner, Barthes and Anthony Burgess, autobiography can be seen as the natural activity of describing the life story of just one individual who is the central character of the life drama as represented in the text. A life is depicted as having developed along both historical and existential axes. An autobiography consists then in a reconstruction that involves a conscious and reflexive elaboration of much of the author's life, including personal and professional experiences. It provides an interpretation of the episodes of a life and the relation the author has to them.

This elaborated construction of a life is the way by which the individual represents those aspects of his or her past that are relevant to the present situation. It consists not just of a collection or litany of all the events in the course of a life, but rather of their shaping by the author's own structural self-images through which he or she conceives of self. An autobiographical text thus presupposes that the person has developed an identity, an individuality and a consciousness in order to organize his or her own personal history from the perspective of the present. Its inner unity is a consequence of the constructive and constitutive activity that is characteristic of personal consciousness. As an idiosyncratic text, it is personal both in its selection of events and in its expression or style.

Though a synchronic reconstruction usually late in life, an autobiography is concerned with the diachronic or longitudinal aspects of personality. In contrast, much social science is involved in a process of amputating the personal from the lived totality. An account of a long journey such as learning to teach cannot be observed merely once or twice in the course of the voyage. More detailed information is needed from many instances over substantial portions of a career. But this long-range perspective may not always be feasible, nor possible. Stringer (1988) offered an exemplary if personal biography entitled 'Fragmentation' by assembling some fragments of allegedly other-authored texts. He concluded, as he might have begun, with the text of Kelly's (1955) fragmentation corollary.

Much of Barthes' (1977) work also proceeded by such techniques of interruption. To write in fragments or notes entails new, non-linear sequences and incoherences that may be quite proper to life itself. Narratives allow meaning but not 'the' meaning to be put into the world. The poetics of experience yield open-ended and polysemic texts so that unified arguments are accompanied by itineraries of topics. The pattern or leading idea of a life is elusive even when the describer is the described. Indeed, as Gide (1967) explained in his journal, writing changes us as it leaves us. Writing modifies the movement of our lives. We are its work.

Berk (1980) searched teachers' educational autobiographies for episodes or moments of insight that provided them with a leap forward. Pinar (1980, 1981a, b) and Grumet (1980) also asked teachers to supply descriptive autobiographical narratives about their childhoods and about their subsequent development (regressive). The central concepts that emerged (analysis) related to the teachers' life structure or to the basic pattern or design of their lives at a given time. The teachers then recorded accounts of their projected futures (progressive) and finally produced statements of self (synthesis).

Pinar and Grumet have sought to build teachers' critical consciousness through self-examination. Pinar (1974, p. 20) named his existential method *currere*, from the Latin infinitive root of curriculum, and explained that it is not the course to be run, or the artefacts employed in the running of the course, 'it is the running of the course . . . our experience of our lives'. The method relies on lived experience and is defined in terms of a number of possible activities outlined in these two concluding chapters: writing an autobiographical account of our own educational experiences; keeping a journal; analysis of our own personal reading; writing a novel based on our own life; and the study of relationships that are revealed as those activities are carried on. The focus is not just on the material contents of the course of teacher education but on the existential experience of studying and living through it.

Kirby (1989), one of my teacher colleagues, prepared a tourist guide to her own teaching. Remembering how in her pre-service teacher education programme she had been discouraged from majoring in special education, her guidebook detailed how a visitor might now prepare for a trip to such a disabled children's developmental unit. In addition to dealing with health, luggage, what to wear and other things, she recommended a happy disposition and a smiling face! She concluded by reviewing her guide as if for publication in a teacher newsletter. Like Pinar (1981b), she believes that we write out autobiography for ourselves and portray our teaching lives to ourselves.

Biography

For Murray (1938) the organism consisted of an infinitely complex series of temporally related activities extending from birth to death. Because of the meaningful connection of sequences, the life-cycle of a single individual should be taken as the long unit of psychology. While it is feasible to study the organism during one episode, this is an arbitrarily selected part of the whole.

'The history of the organism is the organism. This proposition calls for biographical studies' (Murray, 1938, p. 39).

Bannister (1985) was also interested in biography as an opportunity for placing the psychology of a person in the context of his or her time and place. Biography can then reveal not only the nature of the person's subjective definitions and choices, but also raise the issue of consistency of choice throughout a person's life. Bannister showed that it was possible in the context of Ulysses S. Grant's total life to consider the way in which superordinate constructs or major concerns such as loyalty helped make sense out of apparent inconsistencies at a more subordinate or daily level (see Chapter 7).

In contrast, the Brussels method of De Waele and Harré (1979) explored biography through the assisted construction of autobiography so that individuals, such as convicted murderers, volunteered to provide written reports of their own lives, told in their own ways, in order to provide access to their cognitive matrix or organized system for knowledge and action. These 'naive' autobiographical data provided the means for biographical reconstruction and negotiation with the team of researchers. The texts were then investigated through specially designed focusing interviews that consisted of reflexive and direct questions. In seeking to identify the generative mechanisms that gave rise to the behaviour, the relevance of Kelly's dynamic theory was acknowledged.

The heart of the biographer's task is that he or she is interpreting data on the person in order to formulate the central, organizing and animating story of that person's life. As Edel (1978, p. 2) wrote, when the biographer 'can discover a myth, he has found his story. He or she knows the meaning of his [or her] material', which can then be selected and sifted. Student teachers on practice teaching could similarly observe and interview their supervising teachers in order to construct anonymous pedagogical biographies rather than merely writing up routine observation notes of their lessons. The very activity of producing a biography involves a search for coherence and evolution. A life is then seen as an emergent perspective that can never be wholly ripped away from the person who experiences it.

Butt (1984) also argued for the benefits of using biography in understanding and appreciating teacher perspective, particularly when such accounts carry the teachers' own voices. Despite some shaping through the interview procedures, Elbaz (1981) managed to access the practical knowledge of one teacher. The account brings us close to the lived reality of teachers' work by allowing Sarah's own voice to break the silence.

Novels

Bannister, like Luria, specialized in biographical novels. He was a creator and teller of stories in the grand tradition of the men whose biographies he admired such as Grant, Gauguin and Kelly. Bannister was congratulated by

reviewers for refraining from heavy-handed editorializing and authorial pronouncements. He too let his characters' own vocables or voices be heard.
However, Bannister (1988) himself still described novel writing as an exercise
in the controlled elaboration of an author's own personal construct system. For
the person as novelist or reader, a novel packages 'those confrontations which
Kelly thought basic to life, in which we find our forecasts right or wrong or
totally irrelevant' (Bannister, 1988, p. 509). In these stories, Bannister broke
through the bounds of what has been laid down as the established method in
the enclosed discipline of scientific psychology. As a psychologist-biographer,
he listened to the stories that people tell and sought to discern their central,
animating themes.

Diaries

For Allport (1937), the diary was the preferred way of eliciting personal
understanding because it chronicled the contemporaneous flow of public and
private events of significance to the diarist, whether it was da Vinci, Rousseau,
Wittgenstein or Anne Frank. It provided a record of daily striving to record the
ever-changing present and each entry was sedimented into a particular
moment in time. Allport prized the diary because it did not emerge 'all at once'
as reflections on the past. Its current particularity was also expressed in inner,
personal language that spoke to the self, and in the language of the self. This
was a personal kind of language, a largely intimate form for reflecting and
feeling, close to Vygotsky's (1962) 'inner language'.

Three forms of the diary or personal document may be distinguished that are
self-descriptive and consist of self-referred content: the intimate journal (of
Gide or Kafka), the memoir and the log. The journal of introspection or
personal log may be described as a highly personalized and intimate account of
what is happening in the inner and outer worlds of the teacher as learner. It
shows the directions in which the writer is developing and suggests new
avenues for exploration.

One of the aims of the journal is to promote the building of self and to
recognize it as a possible community or confederation where personal self
complements professional self, that is, where the claims of *myself* and the
teacher I am can be reconciled. Teachers require support in order to break
away from old patterns and to seek new pathways. Teachers, like Andrew in
Chapter 3, can describe, delineate and evaluate this process for themselves,
however painful. If excerpts are filed chronologically by the learner, a valuable
record of growth, development and transformation becomes available. These
perceptions about their day-to-day teaching and its learning activities help
personalize teacher education for them.

The memoir is often solicited and consists of a self-portrait about an aspect
of a career that is depicted from a social and historical perspective. The
synchronic aspects of a teaching life could thus be elicited by providing an

account beginning with 'A day in my life as a teacher . . .'. This is a novelistic technique characteristic of James Joyce, Virginia Woolf and William Faulkner. Alternatively, a teacher could be asked to keep a diary over a teaching week. A teacher could be given a booklet with a day allocated to each page with each page perhaps divided into time segments such as before school, during lessons, break or lunch, and after school. Rather than providing the formula of 'who? what? when? where? how? why?', a detailed invitation could be extended:

> We would like you to keep a daily diary to help us get some idea of how you spread your teaching time through a typical week. We are especially interested in the kinds of things you do as a teacher, when you do them, for how long and with what people. As you write your diary please include lesson times and major teaching activities. Also be sure to include the classes and pupils you teach, what you do with them and any meetings you attend or any other duties you perform. You may also want to include some of the thoughts and feelings you had during the day. At the end of the week look over your diary to see if you have described a fairly typical teaching week for you. Please make any comments you want about what you have written.

Since the early days of navigation, logbooks have been used to provide a full and factual account of a ship's voyage by recording details of its performance, speed and daily progress. Researchers have similarly asked teachers to enter their thoughts and feelings, only to find that such log data cannot be as easily provided nor as readily interpreted. Though investigations of teachers' developing perspectives are fraught with methodological problems, logbooks or diaries can provide insights into teachers' quiet processes and bring us close to the action. A journal not only contains case-studies but is itself one. Holly (1983) studied the professional development of seven teachers through their keeping personal–professional journals. These were used as tools for reflection, analysis and self-evaluation. By exploring their own teaching, partial perspectives became more comprehensive.

Letters

Letters written over a period of time and perhaps subsequently collected can help trace, like a diary, the development of a teacher's understandings. However, they are rarely used because of their co-authorship, reflecting both on the author and the intended reader. Allport (1965) collected over a 100 letters written by Jenny to friends over the last 13 years of her life and this collection was also used by Feixas and Villegas (1987) to illustrate a personal construct analysis of autobiographical texts. However, by being distilled in the selection and editing, letters may not provide a complete record. Passages of little interest may be omitted and may leave us wondering what proportion of the entire correspondence the remaining pages of text constitute.

In sociology, the most thorough-going use of letters was found in Thomas and Znaniecki's (1958) *Polish Peasant*, which consisted of 764 letters obtained and printed in 800 pages. These epistolary sources were used inductively by the researchers to arrive at a collective or modal biography as a more or less general characterization of the actual authors. In contrast, Doestoevsky's novels, including his short story, 'A novel in nine letters', each consists of a knot of discrepant stories whose connections are not immediately apparent. Each of the characters are permitted to speak in their own voices with a minimum of interference from the author. Bakhtin described this genre as polyphonic, that is, as having many points of view, many voices each of which is to be given its full due. By encompassing differences in a simultaneity, transformation of perspective can be effected. To move to a dialogic conception of the world is to make a move almost as great as that from a geocentric perspective to a Copernican world view. Much as the earth was moved out of its central or monologic place to accommodate the complex interaction of the Copernican universe, so authors are removed from the centre of the textual world to allow their characters to exert their own forces. A perspective may thus be seen as a process rather than a location.

In an episode consisting of different stances, Kaufman's (1964) novel about beginning teaching, *Up the Down Staircase*, contrasted the first-year teacher's planned lesson notes with her own subsequent account of the actual lesson; then with the observation notes of her supervising head of department; and finally with the class report of a participating student. The key or pivotal questions that she used in the lesson on Frost's poem, 'The road not taken', were: 'What turning point have you had in your life? What choice did you make, and why? How did you feel about your choice later?'

Upon retirement, Rae (1987) wrote and published the letters he wished he had been able to write to parents while a headmaster for the previous 16 years. He wanted parents to understand his point of view as head. In addition, he wanted to write about the practice of education and so relied as far as possible on his own experience. Bradbury (1988) also wrote unsent letters, that might have been sent but never were, to allegedly spare him the trouble of ever having to write an autobiography.

Phillipson (1989) wrote *In Modernity's Wake: The Ameurunculus Letters* as an alleged collection of letters retrieved by out-field workers from the sub-London peat bog. It is 'established' that they were left out for the 'post-man' (or is it 'wake-man'?) immediately preceding the catastrophe that engulfed the West on 16 June 2004. They are addressed to a disparate, largely uncontactable, non-correspondent group, including Heidegger, Derrida and Barthes. Their concern is with arts and artists, post-phenomenology and post-structuralism. Writing is shown as having to gather around itself new criteria such as the provocation of discomfort, self-splitting and the slide out of security.

Like Ameurunculus (and Phillipson), teachers can best speak and write for themselves. Reconstruction of perspective can be aided by their writing about present teaching difficulties and by seeking advice from, for example, former teachers of their own whom they admire. They can then provide those teachers' possible replies. Beginning teachers might also initiate correspondence not directly with themselves but indirectly either with their practice teaching supervisors or with their university tutors.

Interviews, oral testimony, images

Elbaz (1981) and Yonemura (1982) had teachers record and discuss their observations on their teaching practices, while Woods (1985) had teachers talk into the tape-recorder about teaching and their careers. Terkel (1977) spent 20 years conducting radio interviews about the world of work. These envelopes of sound may be described as cues to greater consciousness. Teachers need such opportunities to bring their intuitive knowledge to consciousness for critical evaluation.

Bruner (1987) recorded the oral testimony of four members of a family who were each asked to tell the story of their own lives within 30 minutes. They were told that the researchers were not interested in judging or in 'curing' the family members but rather in how they saw their lives. They were then asked questions for another 30 minutes to get a better picture of how their stories had been put together. The staff of a school or groups of students (see Chapter 5) could also similarly be studied for their communal understandings.

Images can be listened to for their visual voices so that school magazines like a family album can provide photographic or documentary essays, which Barthes (1977) in turn described as family novels. In his own autobiography, he used many family snapshots to illuminate his childhood. Photographs not only allow cultural residues to be collected but also bear the personal imprint of the photographer. When assembled, they can reveal patterns not perceived before about what is going on and what the activities may mean.

One of the films included in Bruner's 'Man: A course of study (MACOS)' followed a Netsilik Eskimo family through the four seasons of a year to produce a deeply felt personal documentary. Carl Rogers took the perhaps more radical step in the early 1940s of filming some of his psychotherapy sessions so that what he did rather than what he said he did could be seen. He brought psychotherapy out into the open. How different present-day theories of teacher education would have been if they too had been based on the actual classroom practice of teachers and their experienced knowledge.

Teaching time-lines

Teachers can sketch their own professional progress by drawing career trajectories. By dividing their time-lines chronologically, from birth to the present year (or to the year of possible retirement), into what are meaningful periods or stages for them, they can explore the changing meaning or pattern of their individual life courses. They can be asked to attend to what they see as the nuclei that opened up or closed off possibilities and even the basic or recurring themes of their sequence of transitions: 'When did they first decide to be a teacher? What lies ahead? What were the crucial events or life-turning points? Was there a transformation? Was it abrupt or gradual?' These significant moments may be described as stepping stones, because, as Kelly (1969, p. 165) explained, the construction of many experiences in an autobiographical account gives such incidents their 'semiotic place' in the chain of events or life contours that follow.

Huberman (1988) drew on Erikson's (1950) eight normative life crises to complete a life-cycle study of 160 secondary school teachers. He asked how they construed their teaching at different moments in their careers; how they viewed other teachers; what were the best years in their teaching; would they choose this career again; and were there moments when they thought of leaving teaching. Clinical and ethnographic interviews of 5 hours were spread over two sessions to encourage greater self-reflection by the teachers.

To the extent that psychological theory is systematically and self-consciously employed to aid in the process of discerning the story, the product may be described as a psychobiography. A psychobiography such as Freud's (1957) of Leonardo da Vinci consists of the systematic use of psychological (especially personality) theory to transform a life into a coherent and illuminating story. For Erikson, the psychosocial story of an individual's life is inherently developmental, typically revealing eight sequential chapters corresponding to stages of growth. He transformed the lives of Gandhi and Luther in order to show how the crises of historical periods could be mirrored in the psychohistories of great men.

Carpenter (1988) used a more dramaturgical or script technique to describe Ezra Pound's succession of masks as including: the troubadour lover, the Whistler dandy, the Barnum showman, the Confucian sage, the learned economist and anti-Semite, the last ant from the broken ant-heap of Europe, Old Gampaw Ez, the certified madman and, lastly, King Lear. Bakhtin was also a master of authorial guises and always searched for new perspectives. In each of their phases, teachers too may be seen as casting off yet another skin and slipping away like William James's crab who never could be quite caught by the claw or category.

In their own voices and in their own hands

A wide range of life-history approaches to self-narrative are available. What the microscope was to biology, personal documentary or storying techniques could be to teaching and teacher education. Narrative helps us to consider the different versions of reality, including which is more 'real', what we think we are, what we want to be, what we are afraid to be, what we pretend to be or what we think others think we are.

Thomson (1985) and his group of teachers moved through the technological periphery of schooling and reported that their diary or journal observations helped them to reflect more effectively on their teaching perspectives even as they taught. It was as if their own video-camera or cassette-recorder was 'on' all the time. Observing and reflecting upon their teaching performance seemed to sharpen their sensitivity to their own practice. They felt that they had improved their capacity to be constructively critical of their own perceptions.

There are many ways in which teachers can learn to understand their own classroom perspectives and thus become their own more self-conscious auto-ethnographers. As shown in Chapter 7, these prompts to narrative perspectives are most useful in the hands of teachers themselves, as tools in their own work of becoming aware of the knowledge they possess, how they use it, and how they might extend it and use it more effectively to further their purposes.

Self-narrative approaches focus on consciousness and represent a decisive change in our view of teacher education and knowledge. As Polanyi (1958, pp. 26–7) wrote, the participation of the knower in shaping his or her knowledge, which was before tolerated only as a shortcoming to be eliminated from perfect knowledge is 'now recognised as the true guide and master of our cognitive powers'. Moments of heightened self-consciousness can lead to a more critical perspective on the world just as a personal conversion or renaissance can produce a new point of view. Teachers' stories and their agendas need to be recovered, remembered, studied, acknowledged and appreciated. Teachers' voices operate as their speaking personality or consciousness to supply the essential clue to the transformation of their perspectives. The evolution of their tone and quality is the particular concern of teacher education.

7

Ways of reflecting upon narrative perspectives

The aim in this concluding chapter is to show that, while teacher narratives or texts are capable of analysis and interpretation from a variety of theoretical perspectives and of involving varying degrees of intrusiveness, they are most properly treated by way of yet another story or through an extended and appreciative response. This resolution arises out of sharing and out of a disciplined subjectivity or attuned intuition (see Chapter 5). Meanings are best assigned by the author-teachers themselves as interpreter-critics of their own pedagogical accounts. They can best be helped to grasp the similarities and differences in the stories that constitute their teaching perspectives.

Freud (1967) chose to respond to one of his own dream texts in order to demonstrate his method of interpretation. In general, he sought to avoid arbitrariness and uncertainty by imposing the task of interpretation upon the dreamer-storyteller him or herself. The concern is not with 'what occurs to the INTERPRETER in connection with a particular element . . . but with what occurs to the DREAMER' (Freud, 1967, p. 130). In Freud's judgement, 'the situation [of analysis] is in fact more favourable in the case of SELF-observation than in that of other people' (p. 137).

The further suggestion in this concluding chapter is that the work of response ought to be brought to bear not only upon the text's bipolar distinctions or constructs, but also upon the text as a whole, that is, upon its structure or connectedness. Accordingly, each construct can be responded to as if the teacher's story were a geological conglomerate in which each fragment merits attention. However, in addition, the whole text can also be appreciated as a complete feature or pinnacle, as a unifying perspective. For James (1890, p. 239), consciousness 'does not appear to itself chopped up in bits. It is nothing jointed; it flows . . . as a river or a stream.' The whole channel has a sense rather than a defined meaning.

Changes in the quality of consciousness as it makes an impression upon itself may take the form of either gradual acquisitions or more dramatic periodic leaps. As transformations of perspective, the latter consist not merely in the gaining of more conceptual knowledge, but in the breaking open of one's old way of seeing. To alter our vision or 'to modify the frame of reference within which we interpret our experience . . . is to modify ourselves' (Polanyi, 1958, p. 105). The portion of self that has been considered in this book is pedagogical, that is, the *teacher I am*. Such a self is a proper concept or construct in that it refers to a group of events that are alike in a certain way and, in that same way, necessarily different from other events. 'The way in which the events are alike is the self. That also makes the self an individual' (Kelly, 1955, p. 131). Having thus been conceptualized, the teacher self was used as an item in the context of superordinate perspectives. The self became one of three or more persons, at least two of whom were alike and different from at least one of the others. The other persons against whom the *teacher I am* was tested included the *teacher I would like to be*, the *teacher I fear to be* and *pupils*. The meaning of self as it was transformed over time was then explored.

As in the previous chapters, a teacher's perspective may be described as a complex intellectual–psycho-social gestalt; that is, as a 'self-rhythmed' (Emig, 1983, p. 126) way of making and unmaking a 'web of meaning' or of posing and opposing a set of personal and professional hypotheses. Transformation consists in the reorganization or reallocation of its interpretive structures in the light of experience. However, the fabrication of any such definition is not subject to the usual kind of critical or scientific dissection – nor is the justification of any evaluation of a preferred way of perceiving the realities of the classroom. While a number of approaches are offered below that attempt to contact the stories that teachers have to tell, to seek also to span form and worthwhileness is an even more perilous enterprise. Whether or not the stories are 'true' is not the problem. 'The only question is whether what I tell is My fable, My truth' (Jung, 1977, p. 17).

Because of the multiple renaissance in the use of narrative approaches, Bertaux and Kohli (1984) do not expect any standard methodology to appear, but accepted instead the need for methodological pluralism in developing procedures to aid in the understanding of individuals and their circumstances. While Sartre (1968) also allowed that works of the mind are tricky and difficult 'objects' to classify, it can be acknowledged that any procedure has a claim to consideration if it can tell us something about the subjective orientations of teachers in their social worlds. Each of the following methods of analysis represents a style of investigating and of understanding human experience, whether by staying close to or by retreating from individual teachers. Three sets of research approaches are discussed. The first contrasts idiographic and nomothetic perspectives, and the second those that are literary and psychological. Finally, storying is seen as a means of responding imaginatively so that transformation becomes possible.

Idiographic or nomothetic approaches

Idiographic procedures seek to pick up on the way individuals express their understanding of the worlds they construct and may or may not include further analysis of these expressions. A nomothetic or second-order perspective requires that the observer-educator as critic orients him or herself towards, subsumes and makes statements about the individual teacher's ideas about the classroom. This distinction has also been drawn in terms of phenomenology versus phenomenography (Marton, 1981), emic versus etic approaches (Pike, 1967) and human versus natural science. Koestler (1976) represented the same contrast as a continuous spectrum of the rainbow stretching from the poet-novelist to the physicist. Though extremes, both are, however, part of the same bipolar construct or enterprise. Both superimpose their own vision of reality on the world of teacher education by selecting and highlighting those aspects that they consider significant and by ignoring others that they find irrelevant. The analysis can thus seek either to grasp the teacher's own personal categories of understanding, options and choices or to measure the teacher against some theory of development in a more normative fashion.

Narrative perspective and its analysis can be used either as part of a dialogue with the teacher or primarily for the teacher educator's own purposes. The former kind of assessment is by self rather than by others, being subjective and experiential. The value of this kind of interpretation rests on the extent to which it can clarify an individual's dilemmas and promote his or her own pedagogical and psychological transformation. The task is then that of reconstructing the author's personal world from his or her own viewpoint by making explicit his or her phenomenal categories, that is, those patterns through which he or she structures his or her world and interprets his or her existence. The teacher's point of view is approached through the structured explication but without judgement of his or her personal constructs.

Existential projects

Allport (1937) advocated an existential approach to analysis that sought to render the individuality of a person which is his or her outstanding characteristic. Accordingly, each teaching life is seen as unique and needs to be studied carefully for its own generalizable patterns, lawful regularities and unique constellation of traits. Kelly (1955) and Bannister and Fransella (1986) provided clinical methods of analysing self-characterizations in terms of their central recurring themes or motifs as expressing their own singular and essential being. According to Fransella (1981), we are not interested in the truth or falsehood of people's views but simply in the ways in which they view themselves and their relationships with others. Her analysis did not rest on the derivation of quotients for pleasure–pain statements, nor on counts of such things as positive and negative statements. No attempt was made to give a detailed analysis of the client's writings. Instead, the aim was to show some of his struggling as he tried to extricate himself from the prison of his own construing. Fransella (1981) sought to gain some insights by listening to 'nature babbling to herself'.

Sartre (1964) also advocated similarly intuitive procedures to explicate an author's existential project so as to render its concrete reality as a lived totalization. The project was depicted as the central statement, the particular essence, the life source, the *raison d'être* or conceptualization that governs the most important choices in the life of the author of the text. The human project in all its profoundity and particularity is known by reflection, but this is difficult to analyse. Words, types of reasoning and methods exist only in limited quantity; among them are empty spaces and misgivings. However, as soon as people speak or write, they also say more and something different from what they want to say; they are caught up in the mystification of words.

Mair (1984) sought to promote the poetics of experience as a way of coping with this dilemma. He sought the imaginative participation of clients rather than his own disengaged observation. Unlike such a human project, the empirical, scientific approach seems to involve a self-denying puritanical concern to make things 'plain, straight, simple, hard, workmanlike, and external. It suggests that things will be done in a certain, right way which denies or rejects self' (Mair, 1984, p. 9). However, if we cannot know the world except as story, we must enter into and find ways of bodying forth the experience of what is happening. The basic questions then to be explored are: 'What am I up to? How can, I, as a teacher, accept responsibility for my own teaching?'

Life history

A life history approach also seeks to focus on the person's subjective interpretation of his or her situation. Accordingly, teachers are seen as problem-solving individuals who can be asked: 'From this text, what seems to be worrying you? What are you trying to do? What are your intentions? What forces you on? What enables or constrains you?' (Plummer, 1983). In their own ways, the teachers may be helped to get at their own human coefficients or unique perspectives as they try to grasp the ways in which they each construct and make sense of their own teaching.

Biography

Perry (1936) searched for the number and range of the essential characteristics or major structural foci in the life of William James and suggested eight dominant trends. Bannister (1985) sectioned the life of Ulysses S. Grant into roughly 10-year intervals to see where and what he was on the eight occasions. The shifts over time and within circumstances revealed a farm boy in Ohio, a smart young hero in the Mexican War, a semi-alcoholic lieutenant in an isolated Californian outpost, an unsuccessful businessman, a door-to-door salesman, the commander of all the Northern forces in the American Civil War, the President of the United States, a dying and bankrupt business proprietor whose partner had embezzled all the funds and, finally, before his death, writing his memoirs to save his family from destitution. However, loyalty remained one of Grant's enduring biographics or forms of psychological inflection. Teachers too may experience many shifts in perspective but still retain a unique focus or embodied outlook.

The task in biography is to subsume someone else's construct system, to select incidents from a life so arranged and linked as to render it intelligible. The biographer seeks to uncover the traces of a person's thinking during a given period in which he or she was involved in, say, the slow process of constructing an original point of view. It is as though a knife cuts through a layer cake or a road is driven through a mountain to reveal its geology. However, biographical methods remain a specialized branch of fiction or invention that explores motivation in the form of an open letter in which the biographer continually asks the subject: 'This is what I think you had at the back of your mind on this or that occasion. How right am I?' Hodges (1983) thus sought for the quality of Turing's experience rather than for mere information about him. The challenge for the biographer is to break the code of a life.

Biography becomes especially Kellyian in approach when intimate documents such as diaries and letters are scrutinized. Personal impressions of contemporaries, including interviews with any still living, are sought and as complete a thematic chronology as possible is constructed. Any writings are analysed as the biographer tries to grasp his or her subjects' view of the world, of marker events and of their views of themselves at different points in their careers. They try to get in tune with their subjects' feelings and emotional life and to render those inner states. However, any biography only exists in order to be rewritten. Constructive alternativism is also itself a cunning in-built device of personal construct psychology. According to Stringer (1985), this prevents its own texts from ever being closed in final definition and, when seen reflexively, this turns their reading into their rewriting.

Content analysis

Content or personal structure analysis is a technique that examines the frequency with which ideas or topics are associated in verbal material. Baldwin (1942) applied this method to the collection of over 100 letters written by Jenny late in her life. She was depicted by Allport (1961) as highly jealous of her son; paranoid concerning her relationships with women; with a strong aesthetic interest; and scrupulous in matters of money. Allport (1965) also later conducted more elaborate computerized analysis of these same letters.

De Waele and Harré (1979) dismembered or reassembled 'naive' autobiography according to a nine-fold thematic scheme based on the Brussels Biographical Inventory. They studied the text for its microsociological framework, the social-psychological life pattern and for individual characteristics relating to self and personality. However, tables of frequencies were not produced. They aimed instead to make each life history event intelligible by locating it in a unique sequential and unfolding process, together with the combination of elements forming the individual's unique stages. They sought to discover the progression within the individual's history of situations, which may constitute a law of his or her life. De Waele and Harré (1979, p. 187) explained that autobiography provides the material for the internal, nomothetic analysis of an idiograph, that is, for 'a representation of a human life'.

Any method of formal content analysis tends to destroy the importance of wholeness. The coding of isolated units ignores the structure of temporal processes and the contextual determinants of the content. Too often the biographer-researcher or the teacher educator as practicum supervisor may impose his or her choice of categories on the material so that it no longer makes explicit the subject of the biography's own first-order constructs. As Lightfoot (1983, p. 255) warned, teachers' voices defy easy categorization and 'cracks [can] appear in facile and anachronistic caricatures'. For example, how can anyone's teaching be evaluated by an outsider as 'fair' or 'outstanding'?

Powell (1985) conducted a content analysis of 22 autobiographical accounts by graduates which showed that, for them, the most enduring effects of their higher education involved learning high-level intellectual skills, attitudes and values of personal and professional significance and factors that helped or hindered learning. However, the evidence produced in support of such an interpretation may be rooted in the observer's own private understanding, which constitutes not the documents of the case but rather unpublishable second-order data. What ought to have been open to scrutiny becomes privatized instead.

While Bertaux and Kohli (1984) believed that the synthetic potential of any life story expresses itself only through the analytic skill of the researcher, his or her searching and probing still remain behind, orchestrating the text. However, in less idiographic approaches to narrative production and analysis, the observer may become an intrusive director rather than a co-author. The researcher asks the original questions and, even if they are later erased, this presence still lurks behind the 'native' autobiography. But intentions are always richer than texts, so that those of the teachers, for example, are always still standing behind their expression. In order to make this personal reality explicit, studies of teachers and their classrooms must become exegetical and autobiographical. Teachers need to excavate those layers of intention and experience that antedate and live below the text which is daily teaching, of which language and events are deposits. As the next major section of this chapter shows, the description of classrooms can be more experiential in a literary way and hence come to mimic less the formalism of many traditional approaches.

Appraisal

Using the most normative approach, Dollard (1935) provided seven criteria for appraising a life history in its various contexts (organic, familial, situational and historical-cultural), which he viewed developmentally or in stages. Dollard deliberately attempted to define the growth of a person in a cultural milieu and to make sense of it within his own theoretical schema, and his personal preference was for a psychodynamic formulation. However, as Kelly (1969) found, the more we understand what is actually happening the less useful may be the lexicon of psychodynamic or second-order terms. A world without doubt, even though thoroughly analysed, may not be possible. Such a normative world would be jam-packed with 'terminal conclusions, . . . lead pipe certainties, dictionary definitive and doomsday finalities' (Kelly, 1969, pp. 51–2).

Teachers may need to learn to fall back on themselves rather than upon the ordered comfort of the words of others in order to make their own unspoken knowledge more articulate, and to uncover their own personal constructs. Instead of wiping the slates clean, they can learn to understand the perspectives of which they are the existential bases and which make their knowing possible. Our life histories are not liabilities to be summarily exorcised but are the precondition for our knowing. Our present projects are situated in our own stories and it is these narratives that offer us opportunities to reconstruct our teaching agendas.

Earle (1977, p. 10) described autobiographical work as raising to reflexive consciousness what is already grasped implicitly, 'excavating the implicit, buried sense of existence of a singular being by that singular being'. In such an ontological autobiography, the emphasis is not upon its recorded character nor upon it as a form of literature, but rather upon it as a form both of consciousness-raising and of deepening and transforming intuition.

Literary and psychological approaches

If the promising analogies in the social sciences are now coming not from the contrivances of physical manipulation but from those of cultural performance, such as in literature, the second set of analytical procedures to be considered derives from literary criticism. According to Bruner (1986), this is not such a bad place to look, as the task of analysing the great texts has formerly fallen to it. This literary mode also serves to remind us that meaning cannot be detached from the uses of language. The following set of approaches range from new criticism through cognitive psychology to personal construct appreciations. Varying emphases are placed on the four elements of author, text, reader and critic. This shift of emphasis represents movement from the supremacy of the text and its critic, through the triumvirate of the text, critic and author to declaring that 'the author is dead – long live the reader', then to the demise of the omniscient critic and finally culminating in a joint stock company representing the claims of all parties (text, author-reader and critic-teacher educator as learner).

New criticism-poetics

Criticism became New when it no longer acknowledged text as merely covert autobiography. It then severed text not only from the author but also from the reader to focus on the work itself – and, of course, on the critic. Brown (1977) proposed aesthetic cognition as providing a logic of discovery. He used the critical poetics to justify these interpretive procedures. Teachers' narratives could by extension be analysed as if they too were poems, novels or plays. The poetics provide a method for comparing teachers' symbol systems by attending to point of view, metaphor and irony. Rather than being interested in a text for what is said, it is critically dissected for tensions, paradoxes, ambivalences and internal organization.

Narrative perspective

A writer can assume three levels of authorial voice or types of position: from Balzac's omniscience through being just one of the cast of characters like Proust's Marcel to being an inferior, incomplete and perplexed waif like a Beckett or a Castenada. Sartre (1964) captured the possible benefits of such an extended use of viewpoint and of exploring our own multiple 'I's'. When there are two of us, author and hero, the latter does not bear the former's name and is referred to only in the third person. 'This sudden "standing aloof" ... delighted me; I was happy to be HE without his entirely being me. He was my puppet, I could bend him to my whims, put him to the test' (Sartre, 1964, p. 93). Autobiography is a particularly interesting type of story because it is reflexive, with the narrator and the central character being one and the same person – but neither is necessarily the same as the author. As in fixed role treatment, the person who teaches and writes is not who is!

Using different points of view allows teachers to experiment with a range of approaches, from those that are authoritarian and rational through to those that are wholly self-referential. Sterne, Beavois, Calvino and Sartre have shown how multiple perspectives may be explored. They produced novels of people trying to write novels that are also simultaneously presentations of what a novel is about, in addition to including the novelist's own self-reflections on the process of writing it. Just as these are meta-books about books, or fictions about fictions, teachers may also learn to teach by writing about their teaching and by varying their perspectives on it. By storying and restorying we can become 'plurivocal' (Barnieh, 1989). As Connelly and Clandinin (1990) have shown, by writing narratively we can sort out whose voice is the dominant one. It may be the *teacher I am*, the *teacher I would like to be* or the *teacher I fear to be*.

Metaphor

Text can be analysed for its 'as if' or metaphoric qualities. Teaching could be depicted either in analogic terms as the activity of an orchestra conductor or in iconic terms as that of a stranger or outsider. A fundamental root metaphor or paradigm might be constructed in which teaching is construed as a language game with the teacher construed either as a post-modern novelist-dramatist or as a Kellyian, constructivist philosopher-psychologist. When left unexamined for too long, metaphors can become myths; however, they can be unfrozen or unmasked by asking the 'right' questions, as for example: 'In what respects are or are not teachers usefully seen as novelistic self-narrators?' Some metaphors – that is, some ways of construing – work better for teachers than others in guiding their search for direction and understanding. Metaphors are most useful when they afford fresh insights and help to create new frames of vision.

Irony

Rather than mirroring the grim gallows humour of a 'tough' anti-hero, irony can serve a self-reflective function for teachers, helping them to cure their 'certain (zones of) blindness' by estranging the taken-for-granted. Thus either a school might be critiqued by comparing it to a custodial institution or the effects of a national curriculum can be exposed by recalling the 'Poor scholar's lament' in which fish had to learn to fly and birds to swim so that in the end they forgot how to swim and fly, respectively!

Silences

A text can be analysed in terms of its gaps and silences so that its contradictions and absences are acknowledged as sources of expression. Macherey (1978) showed that what is important in a story may in reality be what it does not say. Paradoxically, what the text is saying is what it does not say. Absence thus acts as presence. The critic must listen for the silences and search for the hidden agenda. Ravenette (1988) offered a Kellyian interpretation of silences by explaining that any statement needs to be seen in the context of its opposite. It can take on a more precise meaning only when both what is affirmed and what is denied are considered. The contrast is personally representative and logical.

Ideolects

Feixas and Villegas (1987) described their analysis of autobiographical text both as existential-phenomenological and as Kellyian. However, they analysed the first part of Allport's (1965) letters from Jenny by translating it into univocal terms. Using an approach reminiscent of that of Todorov and the Russian formalists, they construed nouns as characters or elements, adjectives as attributes or constructs and verbs as actions. Next, some of Jenny's stylistic resources were deleted. Only the personal elements and their constructions were considered so that the other types of elements were discarded. Only the evaluative and relational constructs were then treated, while those that were behavioural, figurative and descriptive were also discounted. In considering the text only for its quasi-linguistic quality, the Barcelona approach may have succeeded in completely bracketing off the author! By abridging the letters to a limited number of dendograms, further interpretation may be neither encouraged nor possible. Perhaps what they were seeking was Jenny's 'psycholect' or distinctive perspective and this by isolating her 'ideolect' or style as a unique way of using language. However, identifying the key lexical words that an author uses to carry special semantic content may be so disabling that transformation yields to arrestation. Lodge's (1984) fictional novelist, when confronted by his ideolect, never writes again! Silence becomes his perspective.

Structuralist-cognitive approaches

Bruner (1986) explored the structuralist psychology of literature and sought a cognitive analysis of text as world making. By bringing to bear the powerful instruments of psychological, linguistic and literary analysis, he hoped to characterize a text exhaustively in terms of its structure, historical context, linguistic form, genre and multiple levels of meaning (literal, ethical, historical and mystical). A text may achieve its meaning, as Barthes (1974) suggested, in the interplay of the interpretations yielded by different codes, including that of the author. To extract meaning from a text it must be read and interpreted in some multiple way. While Bruner sought to learn more about the author in text as a psychological process, structuralist and formalist approaches may so bracket off the content and author of a text that the actual content of a narrative is seen as no more than its structure. Text is again then considered as an autonomous object. Its reading does not constitute a re-reading or a rewriting.

Genre

Bruner (1986) distinguished three kinds of category systems or aspects of story to capture the attribution process, that is, genre, plot and theme. Genre contrasts third-person, past-tense narratives and epics with first-person, present-tense lyrics. Other ways of organizing the structure of events and their telling include black comedy, the adventure story and fairy tale. These all represent ways that teachers can use to tell about their classrooms.

Epic-Romanesque forms

Bakhtin (1981) provided another sociolinguistic approach by distinguishing between epic and romanesque forms of narrative. In the action world of the epic as perhaps in Jackson's (1968) classroom world, the hero and his perspective do not change, nor does he introspect. In contrast, the romanesque form of, for example, Doestoevsky's *Crime and Punishment* describes a process of self-discovery. This is a problematic world where the self is unstable and where the life story takes the shape of a search for meaning and identity. While some structuralist approaches may seem to refuse to acknowledge the obvious surface meaning of a story and seek instead its deep structures (its parallelism, appositions, inversions, equivalences and its contrasts), Bakhtin (1981) explored the dialogic construction of a text to detect its several voices. In every voice he then could hear two contending voices. The work of building a teacher self is similarly never finished and never definitive.

Plot-theme

The second and third aspects of story concern the interplay of surface plot or of linear sequence with the author's theme or superordinate constructs. As Calvino (1982) explained, a story once could end only in two ways: having passed all the tests, the hero and heroine married or else they died. 'The ultimate meaning to which all stories refer has two faces: the continuity of life, the inevitability of death' (Calvino, 1982, p. 204). For teachers, too, there may have been only rise and fall, success and failure. We can now, however, rescript our fates by adopting other perspectives. Professional renewal can replace 'resignation on the job' and contraction or narrowing of perspective can be offset by vision stretching. By structuring experience in writing, new meanings are able to arise. In devising alternative teaching plots we can reconfigure confused and unformed events and turn them into classroom experience.

Character

The engine of the action in a story may be provided by its characters rather than by a simple plot. The teacher as a hero or heroine can be seen as a helper, a villain, a victim or a false deceiver. Barthes (1977) also stressed the importance of this aspect by admitting that his autobiography must be considered as if it were all spoken by a character in a novel. Romanyshyn (1982) similarly acknowledged that we all construct personal worlds by storying so that, when we each look in the mirror, we never see a visual double of the empirical us standing here on this side of the mirror but rather we see 'A FIGURE IN A STORY. . . . It is a character that I see when I look "in" the mirror' (Romanyshyn, 1982, p. 10).

Teachers might consider their delineation of the characters in their stories by referring to various typologies that depict both types (the archetypical wandering hero, the great mother, the wise old man) and caricatures (a Dickensian Miss Murdstone, a Mr Squeers, a Captain Nemo or a Mr Gradgrind). More recently, Joyce and Proust depicted characters as selves who compete for their roles and earn their rights. Beckett offers individuals who create their own rights as centres of integrity despite the incoherences of life and, like Conrad's 'secret agent', they each become increasingly self-empowering.

For Bruner (1987), the only way to proceed with the analysis of a self-narrative is to plunge directly in and to discover what is realized through what processes. What makes a sentence real for him is the specification of the mental processes that produce it or permit its comprehension. He sought the set of narrative rules that led four family narrators to structure experience in a particular way. Their texts were sampled to see not what they were about but rather how the narrators constructed themselves. He asked: 'To what extent do the sentences take self as an object or as an individual? Are the verbs action-oriented or stative? How many expressions are causative? How linear or convoluted are the accounts? Is the language instrumental or subjunctive? Is it richly adjectival? How frequently are intransitive verbs used like "to seem"?' Such an approach could also help in the study of the joint narrative constructed by a staff of teachers or by a class of students.

Objective hermeneutics

There may be some overlap of Bruner's approach with that of Oevermann's (Terhart, 1982) objective hermeneutics. However, this research group is not interested in the subjective meanings and purposes of individuals but rather only in their own analysis of the deep structural basis or social unconscious of the actors' visible interactions. The materials used are mainly transcriptions from several scenes, as in a family, which are then interpreted in such an extensive manner that a single page leads to 50 pages of interpretation. No detail or subtlety is left unconsidered and every possible variation of 'reading' the text is tried – verification is based not on dialogue with the teachers as narrators but with the researcher-critics themselves. The interpretation with the most explicative power is accepted. However, a definitive interpretation of the 'real' latent meaning structure cannot be produced because the process of interpretation and explication is as endless as is a hall of mirrors. Language and text resist being imprisoned in any one model. No schema can be produced that will encompass all possibilities. In order to understand a text, language in action or personal constructs need to be looked at.

Traves (1988) attempted to tease out the underlying assumptions about language and literature that were contained in a public lecture delivered by Kenneth Baker when British Secretary of State for Education (see Chapter 1). Traves countered the official text by depicting it as trying to conceal fundamental contradictions between the binary opposites that underlay Baker's own political thinking; that is, apparently humane and enlightened appeals to a benign literary heritage (and education) versus the mechanistic version of market forces. Baker praised a teacher as 'coming up with the goods' – itself a telling production line evaluation. Traves saw Baker as exemplifying a 'cultured' common sense together with a bipolar combination of half-digested sub-Leavisite romanticism and of crude utilitarianism. Baker's method was also characterized as moving from one issue to another, picking out potentially attractive ideas, 'latching on to common misconceptions and under-pinning the whole thing with a critical contempt for more rigorous thinking' (Traves, 1988, p. 182).

Interpretation is difficult when a text such as this consists of a series of polemical assertions, anecdotes and veiled references to research. The interpreter too must inevitably reveal his or her own stance in the attempt. Difficult though the task may be, Traves has shown how it is possible to re-read and recast both in opposition to, and beyond, official pronouncements.

Reception theory

Stringer's (1985) title, 'you decide what your title is to be and [read] write to the title', represents an invitation to trial a post-structuralist approach to teacher education. The death of the author allegedly frees the text and the reader from the constraints of his or her prior author-ity. Kelly's suppression of his own references, apart from those to Vygotsky, Adler and Dewey, may also be interpreted as encouraging each reader to be an active producer rather than a mere consumer of the text of personal construct theory. In an authorless text, no single truth-bearing interpretation is specially privileged. It is writable by the readers as they identify their own plurality of meanings.

The focus of recent productive literary theory on texts and readers also encourages teacher educators and researchers to pay more attention to material other than that generated by the traditional Repertory grid or clinical interview, that is, to other human documents such as stories, novels and conversations. Autobiography provides an ideal prompt for teachers to self-reflect, because this enables the teacher self to be construed as a text open to multiple meanings; indeed, as taking its very existence from the various readings by others and self. The attempt to look into the core of a teaching self-narrative may help the writer-reader-author find him or herself there and in the process of epistemologically storying.

Holroyd (1988) mounted a theory of reconstruction to at least partially answer those who like Stringer would completely remove the text from the author in order to give it to the reader to remake entirely. Between the lines of text the invisible lives of the authors may be found and any examination into the implications of these areas may fruitfully disturb the text. The teacher as author still represents a code that teacher educators as readers should possess for clarification of their meanings. To be blind to the unprinted parts of the page is unnecessarily restrictive, even as ignorance of the unconscious may be to a psychoanalyst.

Analysis as response

Using the third or Kellyian set of approaches, Yorke (1987) described a teacher's action perspective as an experiment that requires an explanatory and retrospective analysis. A methodology based on accounts is likely to provide a better fit with his or her constructs than an approach in which the constructs of another person are dominant. The teacher's constructs need to be seen as a relational whole and to be submitted to a hermeneutic process that seeks their deeper significances. The process is hermeneutic in the sense that it is based on the dialectics of part–part and part–whole, which not only spirals in towards a fuller interpretation of what is available but also outwards to seek further evidence.

Hunt (1987) and Ravenette (1988) both acknowledge that teachers' texts can manifest aspects of their consciousness and that a particularly useful role for the teacher educator-critic to adopt is that of collaborative learner and appreciative co-reader. However, this is an arduous role. Hunt's (1951) master's thesis was the first Repertory grid study and also the first in the theory of personal constructs; however, it was too unorthodox, he felt, to be pub-lished. Hunt's work for the next 25 years made no reference to Kelly's theory, which itself was not 'revived' until 1971 with the publication of the first edition of *Inquiring Man* (Bannister and Fransella, 1986). Hunt (1987) reported that he did not know enough about the meaning and implication of 'every person is a psychologist' (p. 10) and that in the early 1950s there was a great deal of faith in 'psychology-as-science (Outside-in)', which would have strongly resisted the 'Inside-out' approach.

Hunt now uses paragraph completion invitations to bring out teachers' implicit theories. These begin with: 'About my work. . . . Reflections about my journal. . . . My concepts of teachers, goals and teaching approaches. . . . My model of teaching or teacher development. . . . My metaphor of teaching. . .'. Four experienced practitioners who were graduate students in his learning styles classes agreed to 'go public' and to allow their implicit theories to appear as examples of beginning with ourselves. Such texts can be analysed by the practitioners themselves in terms of the content, tone, permeability and communicability of their constructs. This serves to increase their self-understanding, to improve communication and to provide a clearer base on which to evaluate suggestions from others or from outside-in information. The foundation is thus laid for changing their own actions.

Hunt's own role is to seek ways of creating open, reciprocal climates in order to enhance the teachers' and his own self-knowledge. Teachers are to be helped to become their own best theorists and indeed, their own best teacher educators. As teacher educators conversely learn to shed their theorist-as-expert role, they can assume the more challenging role of forging collegial relationships with the practitioners – and both can become resources for each other.

Such facilitation requires special expertise such as demonstrated by Connelly and Clandinin (1988). Like Hunt, these two curriculum and narrative theorists do not complete any separate analyses of their teachers' stories because these need to involve the teacher-authors. Some of the questions they consider that could be asked to help teachers gain some distance from and control over their stories include: 'What view of students do I have? Of subject matter? Of teaching? Of the teaching-learning relationship? Of the context in which education happens?' (Connelly and Clandinin, 1988, p. 47). Teachers can be encouraged to think of their teaching experience as a text that they can interpret.

Nicoll (1989), one of my teacher colleagues, adopted a critical posture towards her own teaching self-report and scrutinized it by looking for the functions of her explanations of her teacher self. She found that three themes emerged: her leadership role in setting the mood of her classroom; her relaxed approach to discipline; and her provision of a wide range of learning experiences for her students. Oberg and Underwood (1989) explored their congruent experiences of a curriculum foundations course. They entered their experiences and created for themselves and others an integrated understanding of teacher development and how it may be fostered. With her broader perspective, Oberg seeks the development of her teachers as persons rather than of techniques. Teachers are helped to find a voice and a footing. By imagining their perspectives, they can become prophets of their own pedagogy.

Ravenette (1988) also shares Hunt's long experience in Kellyian procedures and specializes in creative ways of helping teachers find fresh solutions, especially through the use of questions such as: 'What does my writing deny? What does it further imply? What does my answer presuppose? What is the context within which my answer is valid?' (Ravenette, 1988, p. 109). In these ways, the teachers can learn to read carefully the construction of their own teaching experiences in order to sense the bipolarities that they use to sum up and give them meaning. These two poles of the constructs or underlying dimensions of appraisal can be fielded respectively against each other to yield unexpected relations. New dualities or perspectives can be conjured up and the world of teaching reappraised in terms of the teachers' own idiosyncratic logic or personal constructs.

In order to tease out what the classroom problems are, the events have to be disentangled from the constructions the teachers put on them (see Chapter 4). Once the teachers' actions as reported are acknowledged as purposeful, the further question can be asked: 'For what problem is this teaching behaviour a solution?' Teachers' perspectives are at the heart of their teaching and, by exploring their construction of themselves and their circumstances, their transformation can be promoted. A powerful kind of empathy is possible when teacher educators learn to express their understanding of teachers' inner worlds through the use both of the teachers' own vocabularies and of their own personal frames of references.

Stephens (1985) also described the task of trying to work with the actual psychological reality or phenomenal experience of teachers and not with it as reframed, literalized and interiorized by the metaphors of the superior, detached natural scientist. What needs to be adopted is a practice of fidelity to teachers' experience as it takes place or as it is construed as part of their personal worlds. The task consists neither in explanation nor in assessment but in 'imaginal reconstruction' (Romanyshyn, 1982, p. 89). We can learn to understand teachers (and ourselves) by setting them in a story as characters in action.

We all construe from our own perspective and people our own personal stories with our portrayals of self and others. Everyone thinks of their life and all lives as something that can in every sense of the word be told as a 'story'. Stories 'imaginally understood' belong to the character of human psychological life as much as facts empirically understood belong to the character of scientific life. 'One's own life and the life of another MAKES SENSE psychologically as a story. They do not make sense because we know all the facts' (Romanyshyn, 1982, p. 89).

Telling a story by way of response is a challenging procedure for illuminating the joint exploration of teachers' professional practice. It is part of the effectiveness of the story as a technique that it simultaneously reaches the head, heart and intentions of the teacher yet leaves him or her free to construct yet another new version and perhaps a new course of action. In Kelly's (1955) fixed role treatment, the teacher is not asked to believe or do anything or to change in any particular way once he or she has read the alternative scenario or story. Any change that does take place is of his or her own devising. This may well be the most difficult of all analytic approaches, as it depends upon a subsequent synthetic stage in which the teacher educator as learner must demonstrate a powerful grasp of each teaching problem. The relevant story must speak directly to the teacher, to his or her particular classroom and situation. A storytelling approach goes far beyond orthodox psychological theories and points to an intuitive understanding. The question of who is teacher educator and who is teacher becomes less the question as we concern ourselves, as Connelly and Clandinin (1990) have advised, with questions of collaboration, trust and relationship as we live, story and restory our collaborative research of life.

In Chapter 4, we met Fay who was in her second year of teaching. Here is her initial self-narrative written in the form of a teaching sketch.

As a teacher of English, Fay feels there are many areas of concern in her own teaching methods and content that need attention. There seems to be so much the students have to know that is difficult to choose material that is appropriate for them. Often she is not quite sure if the method being used is effective, wasting time, or counter-productive. When viewed at different times, she forms different opinions on this.

Within the classroom, she is aware of certain deficiencies, and, according to mood, irritability, and pressure, remedies these when convenient:

1   supervision of individual students' work – is it close enough?
2   individual attention
3   'reinforcing' after giving back essays, comprehension, set work (drawing on errors and using these to show better ways of writing).

Generally, she is concerned to see that each student does as well as he can (most of the time), and derives a great deal of pleasure from seeing a student master a particular technique. It is often found that a lot of problems that cause dissatisfaction are caused by lack of preparation for that particular period: not reading something carefully enough. This often leads to misunderstanding, which then, in turn, leads to irritability.

With regards to certain areas, having never been taught 'how to teach English' she finds a lot of difficulty as in poetry and creative writing. How does somebody motivate and stimulate students so that they feel inspired to write a piece (from their own desire)? She feels there must be better ways of teaching certain topics – how does one teach grammar and punctuation in an interesting manner? What are the more interesting ways of teaching children how to write?

Books reviews seem to be a big bugbear – no matter how she attempts to teach how to write reviews (she has tried many levels), only those who are capable write satisfactory reviews. She feels that she should be a lot stricter on her classes – making them hand in rough copies, correcting, rewriting, etc. – all this is time-consuming. She would like to be able to get students to analyse a book/article and read between the lines, but is not sure how to go about it.

Another area of concern is trying to get students to communicate orally in front of a class. Oral assessment in the form of an impromptu talk, prepared talk, conversations, dialogues. Her lessons seem to be dull and uninteresting – and time-consuming.

Here is my storying response which invited Fay to adopt, at best temporarily, the teaching story of a make-believe teacher, Carole Spencer. Both texts live by having come into dialogic contact with each other in context.

As a teacher of English, Carole Spencer relishes being with people – the other learner teachers and her own developing classes. She really looks forward to hearing what her pupils can share with her and their friends as they talk to their classes. Her year tens have really responded to their re-enactment of the trial in *To Kill a Mockingbird*. As they swapped the written versions of their roles, her resident punctuation and spelling committee of experts were invaluable. One class prepares a regular spelling test – she writes her answers on the OHP and then the class helps her to correct her answers. They really learned a lot when she wrote on one of her own essay topics right in front of them – all in the heat of creation! Carole has a wide variety of her own interests, and naturally recommends and personally endorses books (and music) she has enjoyed. She infects her classes with her delight in reading by always reading aloud an exciting passage from a favourite novel (or recounting a film version of it) or rendering a short lyric that captures some of her own recent feelings.

A lot of writing flows from all the talking and shared reading. They often collaborate in preparing different versions of the beginning or conclusion of, or omitted scenes from, the class novel. Carole often discusses her classroom 'try-outs' with other teachers They also share in planning a coming unit of work or test. This stimulates and lessens her preparation. She found Stephen Judy's twenty-two alternatives to the study of grammar very helpful, and is turning her classes onto a greater awareness of their language and that of the media. Herbert Kohl's book, *Reading, How To* (Open University Press), was a real breakthrough. She heard about it first through the English Teachers' Association. Carole is always doing new things in her teaching. Most of all, she keeps involving her classes, touching their personal concerns with her teaching. Of course, not everything works – just most of it!

The development of such tailor-made and carefully designed stories and sketches can be a powerful tool in aiding the formation of new teacher perspectives. Kelly (1955, p. 162) described this approach as 'amazingly [having] escaped systematic treatment'. He found it relatively easy to develop new constructs for people in connection with story elements that thus gave them form, definition and usefulness. The composition and playing out of artificial roles also uses fresh elements to develop new constructs. 'The tender shoots of new ideas (are prevented) from being trampled in the frantic rush' (Kelly, 1955, p. 162) to maintain a previous teaching role. The teacher is not 'playing for keeps' and novel constructs are merely 'being tried on for size'. The seeing of constructs as proposed representations of reality rather than reality itself is conducive to experimentation.

I am myself alone

In teacher education we can all develop stories, which further the growth or transformation of our provisional concepts and understandings, in order to promote teaching that is more likely to be relevant and effective. Generalization is not the goal of such interpretive inquiry. The approach requires that we treat every teaching situation as fresh, emergent and filled with mutliple and often contradictory meanings – especially our own. Teaching needs to become more of a permissive space where we are all encouraged to be more relaxed and exploratory.

What teachers may need is not another summary of research findings but a story or a scenario to give them a fresh approach, something to 'facilitate the composed anticipation of contingent events' (Kelly, 1969, p. 55). By entertaining alternatives, the problem can be put into a new perspective. What is important is not that the story gives them 'the' true or authentic way to teach, but rather that it invites them to 'try a new way, calculated and venturesome, and to appraise its outcomes' (p. 64). We can make sense of a person, including ourselves, by setting him or her or us in a story.

As the eventual fashioners of their own stories and perspectives, teachers need to be always on the lookout for new viewpoints. As viewers, they are always the other essential and subjective aspect of what is observed. Each of them needs to discover new dimensions of perception in the struggle to teach. The challenge is to replace the false idea of one fixed point of view that is locked within the limits of one human perspective with another cluster that consists of the juxtaposition of many points of view, each of which is seeking its enlargement.

A teacher's career cycle can be thought of as a series of stories, condensing over time to form a richly idiosyncratic novel, one whose messages we all need to learn to listen for. And encouraging teachers to take a more central role in the making of their classroom stories and to accept their relative autonomy over their teaching does not constitute an overly romantic view. Emancipatory self-knowledge increases teachers' awareness of, and responsibility for, the contradictions contained within their everyday teaching. As Lather (1986) argued, this approach draws attention to the possibilities for transformation inherent even in the present configuration of social processes. In the end, teachers will change schools by understanding themselves. Individual transformation of perspective may represent the epistemological breakthrough needed to ensure that schooling and teacher education are dedicated to the pursuit of individuals and to 'myself alone'.

People change things through changing themselves first and they accomplish their concerns, if at all, only by paying the price of altering themselves. As Sartre (1968) allowed, there are layers of mediation between our personal lives and social processes so that teachers, for example, 'can move from concrete life stories to fundamental social issues' (Bertaux and Kohli, 1984, p. 221). Oberg encouraged one of her teacher colleagues to recreate his professional auto-biography. By transforming the way he understood himself and others, he transformed the way he perceived his institutional and social context and thus transformed his potential for action in that context (Oberg and Blades, n.d.). Consciousness is not interiority. Instead, 'embodied, thrusting into the lived and perceived, it opens out to the common' (Greene, 1988, p. 21). Human consciousness is always situated and the situated teacher is inevitably engaged with other people and reaches out to the world from a particular vantage point.

Conclusion

In this book I have construed the major aim of teacher education as the promotion of teachers' fullest understanding of their individual pedagogic frameworks. The distinctive theme of pre- and in-service programmes can thus be stated as the transformation or rebuilding of teachers' perspectives through the close and collaborative study of their own teaching experiences. Just as Dewey (1938, p. 64) insisted that 'there is no intellectual growth without some reconstruction, some reworking', progressive shifts in personal theories may be necessary for a growing appreciation of the classroom. By adopting approaches that are based both on personal construct and self-narrative procedures, teachers can be helped first to recover and then to reconstrue both their distinctive and their shared teaching life histories. In this book, teachers are encouraged and enabled to identify and interrogate, to scout and to discard their limiting constructs and their self-defeating stories.

Although we have generally been tied to static notions of conceptual structure (Mair, 1977), ways have been shown in the above chapters of representing the intricate, interweaving functioning of individuals in action as they strive to organize and control their teaching. Using Kelly's theory of personal constructs, various artistic analogies and case study material, teacher development has been depicted as consisting of the critical retheorizing of teaching, which is achieved through the reconstruction of meaning structures. Jakobson (1971) has provided another conceptual tool that allows us to construe such changes invitationally in musical or literary historical terms, that is, by representing them as changes of the dominant. The dominant or the focusing component is then seen as the superordinate construct that rules and transforms the remaining components or subordinate constructs in the conceptual system. Loh and Diamond (1989) found that the superordinate constructs of five history teachers operated as guiding messages which in turn helped them to discern the coherent and explanatory narratives that were animating these teaching lives.

It is the dominant that guarantees the distinctiveness of the superstructure and the feel of the recurring scenario. The conceptual evolution of such structures consists of a shift in the hierarchy, so that the whole becomes reordered. It is not so much the disappearance of certain elements and the emergence of others, as it is a question of shifts in the mutual relationships among the components of the system, such as among *myself*, the *teacher I am*, the *teacher I want to be*, the *teacher I fear to be* and *pupils* (see Chapters 3 and 4). With shifts in the dominant, elements, such as *pupils*, which might have originally been seen as secondary become primary and essential, while others which might have been dominant, such as *administrators*, become subsidiary and even optional. The preferred perspective or way of projecting reality onto the classroom shifts as it is re-cognized. There is a shift in the centre of gravity.

The chief resource that teachers bring to teaching is not simply the skills that they have acquired in their training but instead it is themselves, the people they are, the viewpoints that they have adopted. Teachers can each learn to be scholars of their own consciousness and experts in the remodelling of their experiencing of the experience of teaching. A teaching life thus comes to consist of a creativity cycle, a continuous progression of provisional supposition and experiment, exploration and explication, surmise and closure, looseness and tightness, of learning and relearning, of incumbent and challenging hypotheses.

Such a life consists of successive formation and transformation, composition and decomposition, of dominant and tonic. In this book, suggestions have been made as to how variations can be introduced, how teachers as individuals and as groups can reconsider their old ideas and entertain new hopes for the future. Struggling towards a personally negotiated coherence and charting its eventual redirection is preferable to settling for any rigidly imposed order. In his biography of the thought and character of William James, Perry (1936) described all neat schematisms with permanent and absolute distinctions as violating the concreteness of life with all its muddle and struggle. There is always an 'ever not quite' (Perry, 1936, p. 386) to all our formulae and pidgeon holes, with novelty and possibility forever breaking in. Teachers are neither more nor less than their way of understanding their universe. Central to that understanding is the interpretive choices they make in locating themselves within that universe.

References

Adams-Webber, J. and Mirc, E. (1976). Assessing the development of student teachers' role conceptions. *British Journal of Educational Psychology*, 46, 338–80.

Allport, G. W. (1937). *Personality: A Psychological Interpretation*. New York, Holt.

Allport, G. W. (1961). *Pattern and Growth in Personality*. New York, Holt.

Allport, G. W. (1965). *Letters from Jenny*. New York, Harcourt Brace.

Bakan, D. (1974). *On Method: Toward a Reconstruction of Psychological Investigation*. San Francisco, Jossey-Bass.

Baker, K. (1988). *History of English Verse*. London, Faber.

Bakhtin, M. M. (1981). *The Dialogic Imagination*. Austin, University of Texas Press.

Baldwin, A. C. (1942). Personal structure analysis: A statistical method for investigation of the single personality. *Journal of Abnormal and Social Psychology*, 37, 163–83.

Bannister, D. (1981). Knowledge of self. In D. Fontana (ed.), *Psychology for Teachers*, pp. 252–64. London, British Psychological Society.

Bannister, D. (1985). Personal construct theory and the teaching of psychology. *Psychology Teaching*, 13, 2–14.

Bannister, D. (1988). A PCP view of novel writing and reading. In F. Fransella and L. F. Thomas (eds), *Experimenting with Personal Construct Psychology*, pp. 509–14. London, Routledge.

Bannister, D. and Fransella, F. (1986). *Inquiring Man*. London, Croom Helm.

Barnieh, Z. (1989). *Understanding Playwrighting for Children*. University of Calgary.

Barthes, R. (1974). *S/Z: An Essay*. New York, Hill and Wang.

Barthes, R. (1977). *Roland Barthes* (R. Howard transl.). London, Macmillan.

Becker, H. S., Geer, B., Hughes, E. L. and Strauss, A. L. (1961). *Boys in White*. Chicago, Ill., University of Chicago Press.

Berk, L. (1980). Education in lives: Biographic narrative in the study of educational outcomes. *Journal of Curriculum Theorizing*, 2, 88–155.

Bertaux, D. and Kohli, R. (1984). The life story approach: A continental view. *Annual Review of Sociology*, 10, 251–37.

Blake, W. (1805). The Mental Traveller. In W. H. Stevenson (ed.), *The Poems of William Blake* (1971 edition), pp. 578–81. London, Longman.

Bloom, A. (1988). *The Closing of the American Mind*. Harmondsworth, Penguin.

Bobbit, F. (1913). The supervision of city schools. *Twelfth Yearbook of the National Society for the Study of Education*, Part 1. Bloomington, Ill., NSSE.

Bonarius, J. C. J. (1970). Fixed role therapy. *British Journal of Medical Psychology*, 43, 213–19.

Borthwick, J. (1989). Becoming a teacher: Intending teachers' constructs of the experience of pre-service teacher education. Unpublished Ph.D. thesis, Department of Education, University of Queensland, Brisbane.

Bradbury, M. (1988). *Unsent Letters*. London, Deutsch.

Britton, J. (1970). *Language and Learning*. Harmondsworth, Penguin.

Britton, J. (1975). Language and learning. In A. Bullock, *The Bullock Report: A Language for Life*. London, HMSO.

Britton, J. (1987). Vygotsky's contribution to pedagogical theory. *English in Education*, 21, 22–6.

Brown, R. H. (1977). *A Poetic for Sociology: Toward a Logic of Discovery for the Human Sciences*. Cambridge, Cambridge University Press.

Bruner, J. (1986). *Actual Minds: Possible Worlds*. Cambridge, Mass., Harvard University Press.

Bruner, J. (1987). Life as narrative. *Social Research*, 54, 11–32.

Bullock, A. (1975). *The Bullock Report: Language for Life*, London, HMSO.

Butt, R. L. (1984). Arguments for using biography in understanding teacher thinking. In R. Halkes and J. K. Olson (eds), *Teacher Thinking*, pp. 95–102. Lisse, Swets and Zeitlinger.

Calderhead, J. (1988a). The contribution of field experiences to student primary teachers' professional learning. *Research in Education*, 40, 33–49.

Calderhead, J. (1988b). Conceptualizing and evaluating teachers' professional learning. Paper presented at the Research in Teacher Education Workshop, Moray House College of Education, Edinburgh.

Calvino, I. (1982). *If on a Winter's Night a Traveller*. London, Picador.

Carpenter, H. (1988). *A Serious Character: The Life of Ezra Pound*. London, Faber.

Combs, A. W. (1965). *The Professional Education of Teachers*. Boston, Allyn and Bacon.

Combs, A. W. (1972). Some basic concepts for teacher education. *Journal of Teacher Education*, 22, 286–90.

Connelly, F. M. and Clandinin, D. J. (1988). *Teachers as Curriculum Planners: Narratives of Experience*. New York, Teachers College Press.

Connelly, F. M. and Clandinin, D. J. (1990). Stories of experience and narrative inquiry. *Educational Researcher*, 19, 2–14.

Coulter, F. (1987). Affective characteristics of student teachers. In M. J. Dunkin (ed.), *The International Encyclopedia of Teaching and Teacher Education*, pp. 589–98. New York, Pergamon Press.

Crockett, W. H. and Meisel, P. (1974). Construct connectedness, strength of disconfirmation and impression change. *Journal of Personality*, 42, 290–9.

Dawkins, J. S. (1987). *Higher Education: A Policy Discussion Paper*. Canberra, Australian Government Publishing Service, DEET.

Dawkins, J. S. (1988a). *Report of the Committee on Higher Education Funding: Overview and Recommendations*. Canberra, Australian Government Publishing Service, DEET.

Dawkins, J. S. (1988b). *Strengthening Australia's Schools: A Consideration of the Focus and Content of Schooling*. Canberra, Parliament House, DEET.

Day, C. W. (1984). Teachers' thinking – intentions and practice. In R. Halkes and J. K. Olson (eds), *Teacher Thinking: A New Perspective on Persisting Problems in Education*. Lisse, Swets and Zeitlinger.

De Waele, J.-P. and Harré, R. (1979). Autobiography as a psychological method. In G. P. Ginsburg (ed.), *Emerging Strategies in Social Psychological Research*, pp. 177–224. London, John Wiley.

Dewey, J. (1938). *Education and Experience*. New York, Collier Books.

Dewey, J. (1950). *Democracy and Education*. New York, Macmillan.

Diamond, C. T. P. (1979). The constructs, classroom practices and effectiveness of grade ten teachers of written expression. Unpublished Ph.D. thesis, Department of Education, University of Queensland, Brisbane.

Diamond, C. T. P. (1982a). You always end up with conflict: An account of constraints in teaching. In R. D. Eagelson (ed.), *English in the Eighties*, pp. 31–43. Sydney, Australian Association for the Teaching of English.

Diamond, C. T. P. (1982b). Teachers can change: A Kellyian interpretation. *Journal of Education for Teaching*, **8**, 163–73.

Diamond, C. T. P. (1983a). How to succeed in composition: 'Large as life, and twice as natural'. In R. Arnold (ed.), *Timely Voices*, pp. 96–110. Melbourne, Oxford University Press.

Diamond, C. T. P. (1983b). The use of fixed role treatment in teaching. *Psychology in the Schools*, **20**, 74–82.

Diamond, C. T. P. (1985a). Becoming a teacher: An altering eye. In D. Bannister (ed.), *Issues and Approaches in Personal Construct Theory*, pp. 15–35. London, Academic Press.

Diamond, C. T. P. (1985b). Fixed role treatment: Enacting alternative scenarios. *Australian Journal of Education*, **29**, 161–73.

Diamond, C. T. P. (1988a). Benchmarks for progress or teacher education on the rails. *Australian Educational Researcher*, **15**, 1–7.

Diamond, C. T. P. (1988b). Turning on teachers' own constructs. In F. Fransella and L. F. Thomas (eds), *Experimenting with Personal Construct Theory*, pp. 175–84. London, Routledge & Kegan Paul.

Diamond, C. T. P. (1990). An essential perspective: Reconstructing and reconstruing teachers' stories. *International Journal of Personal Construct Psychology*, **3**, 63–76.

Dollard, J. (1935). *Criteria for the Life History: With Analysis of Six Notable Documents*. New Haven, Conn., Yale University Press.

Donaldson, M. (1978). *Children's Minds*. London, Fontana.

Dow, G. (1979). *Learning to Teach: Teaching to Learn*. London, Routledge & Kegan Paul.

Dow, G. (ed.) (1982). *Teacher Learning*. London, Routledge & Kegan Paul.

Earle, W. (1977). *Autobiographical Consciousness: A Philosophical Inquiry into Existence*. Chicago, Ill., Quadrangle Books.

Easterby-Smith, M. (1980). The design, analysis and interpretation of Repertory grids. *International Journal of Man–Machine Studies*, **13**, 3–24.

Edel, L. (1978). Biography: A manifesto. *Biography*, 1, 1–3.
Elbaz, F. (1981). The teacher's 'practical knowledge': Report of a case study. *Curriculum Inquiry*, 11, 43–69.
Eliot, T. S. (1944). *Four Quartets*. London, Faber.
Elvin, L. (1987). *Encounters with Education*. London, Institute of Education, University of London.
Emig, J. (1983). *The Web of Meaning*. Montclair, N.J., Boynton/Cook.
Eraut, M. (1987). Inservice teacher education. In M. J. Dunkin (ed.), *The International Encyclopedia of Teaching and Teacher Education*, pp. 730–43. New York, Pergamon Press.
Erikson, E. (1950). *Childhood and Society*. New York, W. W. Norton.
Feiman-Nemser, S. (1983). Learning to teach. In L. S. Shulman and G. Sykes (eds), *Handbook of Teaching and Policy*, pp. 150–70. New York, Longman.
Feixas, G. and Villegas, M. (1987). Personal construct analysis of autobiographical texts: The case of Jenny. Paper presented at the Seventh International Congress on Personal Construct Psychology, Memphis.
Fransella, F. (1981). Nature babbling to herself: The self-characterization as a therapeutic tool. In H. Bonarius, R. Holland and S. Rosenberg (eds), *Personal Construct Psychology: Recent Advances in Theory and Practice*, pp. 219–30. London, Macmillan.
Freud, S. (1957). Leonardo da Vinci and a memory of his childhood. In J. Strachey (ed. and transl.), *The Standard Edition of the Complete Psychological Works of Sigmund Freud*, Vol. II, pp. 59–137. London, Hogarth Press.
Freud, S. (1967). *The Interpretation of Dreams* (J. Strachan, ed. and transl.). New York, Avon.
Fuller, F. F. (1969). Concerns of teachers: A developmental conceptualization. *American Educational Research Journal*, 6, 207–26.
Gide, A. (1967). *Journals 1889–1949* (J. O'Brien, ed. and transl.). Harmondsworth, Penguin.
Glassberg, S. and Oja, S. N. (1981). A developmental model for enhancing teachers' personal and professional growth. *Journal of Research and Development in Education*, 14, 59–70.
Grant, C. A. and Zeichner, K. M. (1981). In-service support of first year teachers. *Journal of Research and Development in Education*, 14, 99–111.
Greene, M. (1978). The question of personal reality. *Teachers College Record*, 80, 23–35.
Greene, M. (1984). How do we think about our craft? *Teachers College Record*, 86, 55–67.
Greene, M. (1988). *The Dialectic of Freedom*. New York, Teachers College Press.
Gregory, R. L. (1966). Psychology: Towards a science of fiction. *New Society*, 23 May.
Grumet, M. (1980). Autobiography and reconceptualization. *Journal of Curriculum Theorizing*, 2, 155–8.
Habermas, J. (1971). *Knowledge and Human Interests*. London, Heinemann.
Hardy, B. (1987). The nature of narrative. In *The Collected Essays of Barbara Hardy*, pp. 1–13. New Jersey, Barnes & Noble Books.
Heath, R. W. and Neilson, M. A. (1974). Performance based teacher education. *Review of Educational Research*, 44, 463–84.
Hesse, H. (1929). *Steppenwolf* (B. Creighton, transl., 1963 edition). New York, Holt.

Hirsch, E. D. (1987). *Cultural Literacy*. Boston, Mass., Houghton Mifflin.

HMI (1982). *The New Teacher in School*. London, HMSO.

HMI (1983). *Teacher Quality*. London, HMSO.

HMI (1987). *Quality in Schools: The Initial Training of Teachers*. London, HMSO.

Hodges, A. (1983). *The Enigma of Intelligence*. London, Allen & Unwin.

Holly, M. L. (1983). Teacher reflections on classroom life. *Australian Administrator*, 4, 1–6.

Holroyd, M. (1988). A theory of reconstruction. In E. Homberger and J. Charmley (eds), *The Troubled Face of Biography*, pp. 94–103. London, Macmillan.

Huberman, M. (1988). Teacher careers and school improvement. *Journal of Curriculum Studies*, 20, 119–32.

Hunt, D. E. (1951). Studies in the role concept repertory: Conceptual consistency. Unpublished master's thesis, Columbus, Ohio, Ohio State University.

Hunt, D. E. (1978). Teachers are psychologists, too. *Canadian Psychological Review*, 17, 210–18.

Hunt, D. E. (1987). *Beginning with Ourselves: In Practice, Theory and Human Affairs*. Cambridge, Mass., Brookline Books.

Ingvarson, L. and Greenway, P. (1984). Portrayals of teacher development. *Australian Journal of Education*, 28, 45–65.

Jackson, P. W. (1968). *Life in Classrooms*. New York, Holt.

Jacoby, R. (1987). *The Last Intellectuals: American Culture in the Age of Academe*. New York, Basic Books.

Jakobson, R. (1971). *Fundamentals of Language*. The Hague, Mouton.

James, W. (1890). *The Principles of Psychology*, Vols 1 and 2. New York, Holt.

James, W. (1892). *Psychology: The Briefer Course*. New York, Henry Holt.

James, W. (1913). *Talks to Teachers on Psychology*. London, Longman.

Jarrell, R. (1964). *The Bat Poet*. New York, Collier.

Jaynes, J. (1979). *The Origin of Consciousness in the Breakdown of the Bicameral Mind*. London, Allen Lane.

Johnson, M. L. (1988). Hell is the place we don't know we're in: The control-dictions of cultural literacy, strong reading, and poetry. *College English*, 50, 309–17.

Joyce, B. H. (1975). Conceptions of men and their implications for teacher education. In K. Ryan (ed.), *Teacher Education: The Seventy-Fourth Yearbook of the National Society for the Study of Education*, pp. 111–45. Chicago, Ill., University of Chicago Press.

Joyce, B. H. and Clift, R. (1984). The Phoenix agenda: Essential reforms in teacher education. *Educational Researcher*, 7–18.

Joyce, B. H., Howey, K. and Yarger, S. (1976). *Issues to Face: In-service Teacher Education*. Palo Alto, Calif., Education, Research and Development Centre.

Jung, C. G. (1977). *Memories, Dreams, Reflections* (A. Jaffe, ed. and R. and C. Winston, transl.). London, Collins.

Karst, T. O. and Trexler, L. D. (1970). Initial study using fixed-role therapy. *Journal of Consulting and Clinical Psychology*, 34, 762–6.

Kaufman, B. (1964). *Up the Down Staircase*. New York, Avon.

Kelly, G. A. (1955). *The Psychology of Personal Constructs*, Vols 1 and 2. New York, W. W. Norton.

Kelly, G. A. (1969). In B. Maher (ed.), *Clinical Psychology and Personality*. New York, John Wiley.

Kelly, G. A. (1970). A brief introduction to personal construct theory. In D. Bannister (ed.), *Perspectives in Personal Construct Theory*, pp. 1–29. London, Academic Press.

Kelly, G. A. (1977). The psychology of the unknown. In D. Bannister (ed.), *New Perspectives in Personal Construct Theory*, pp. 1–19. London, Academic Press.

Kingman, J. (1988). *Report of the Committee of Inquiry into the Teaching of English Language*. London, HMSO.

Kirby, M. (1989). The accidental teacher: A guide for the educational tourist. Unpublished paper, Department of Education, University of Queensland, Brisbane.

Knowles, J. G. (1987). What student teachers' biographies tell us: Implications for pre-service teacher education. Paper presented to the Conference of the Australian and New Zealand Associations for Research in Education, University of Canterbury, New Zealand.

Koestler, A. (1976). Opening address. Conference, PEN Worldwide Association of Writers. London, 24 August. Reprinted in *The Times*, 25 August 1976.

Lakatos, I. (1968). *The Problem of Inductive Logic*. Amsterdam, North-Holland.

Lather, P. (1986). Research as praxis. *Harvard Educational Review*, 56, 257–77.

Lee, H. (1960). *To Kill A Mockingbird*. Philadelphia, J. B. Lippincott.

Lightfoot, S. L. (1983). The lives of teachers. In L. S. Shulman and G. Sykes (eds), *Handbook of Teaching and Policy*, pp. 241–60. New York, Longman.

Lodge, D. (1984). *Small World*. Harmondsworth, Penguin.

Loh, G. and Diamond, C. T. P. (1989). 'Blips of Meaning': The transformation of readers and history text. *Singapore Journal of Education*, 10, 35–42.

Lunt, P. K. and Livingstone, S. M. (1989). Psychology and statistics. *The Psychologist*, 12, 528–31.

McNamara, D. (1984). Research in teacher education. In R. J. Alexander, M. Croft and J. Lynch (eds), *Change in Teacher Education*, pp. 284–99. London, Holt.

Macherey, P. (1978). *A Theory of Literary Production* (G. Wall, transl.). London, Routledge & Kegan Paul.

Mair, J. M. M. (1977). Metaphors for living. In A. W. Landfield (ed.), *The Nebraska Symposium on Motivation: Personal Construct Theory*, pp. 243–90. Lincoln, University of Nebraska Press.

Mair, J. M. M. (1984). *Towards a Poetics of Experience*. Crichton Royal, Dumfries. Department of Psychological Services and Research.

Mair, J. M. M. (1987). Psychology as story telling. Paper presented at the Seventh International Congress on Personal Construct Psychology, Memphis.

Marton, F. (1981). Phenomenography – Describing conceptions of the world around us. *Instructional Science*, 10, 177–200.

Melville, H. (1851). *Moby Dick* (1981 edition). Berkeley, Calif., University of California Press.

Mezirow, J. (1978). Perspective transformation. *Adult Education*, 28, 100–10.

Mezirow, J. (1981). A critical theory of adult learning and education. *Adult Education*, 32, 3–24.

Mezirow, J. (1989). 'Transformation theory and social action'. *Adult Education Quarterly*, 39, 169–75.

Mezirow, J., Darkenwald, G. G. and Knox, A. (1975). *Last Gamble on Education*. Washington, DC, Adult Education Association of the USA.

Murray, H. A. (1938). *Explorations in Personality*. New York, Oxford University Press.

Neimeyer, R. A. (1985). *The Development of Personal Construct Psychology*. Lincoln, University of Nebraska Press.

Nias, J. (1989). Teaching and the self. In M. L. Holly and C. S. Mcloughlin (eds), *Perspectives on Teacher Professional Development*, pp. 155–71. London, Falmer Press.

Nicoll, C. (1989). Through the looking glass. Unpublished paper, Department of Education, University of Queensland, Brisbane.

Nolte, W. H. (1966). *H. L. Mencken: Literary Critic*. Middletown, Conn., Wesleyan University Press.

Oberg, A. (1986). Using construct theory as a basis of research into teacher professional development. *Journal of Curriculum Studies*, **19**, 55–65.

Oberg, A. and Blades, C. (n.d.) The sound of silence: Reflections of a teacher. Unpublished paper, Victoria, University of Victoria.

Oberg, A. and Underwood, S. (1989). Facilitating teacher self-development: Reflections on experience. Paper, Toronto, Ontario Institute for Studies in Education.

Perry, R. B. (1936). *The Thought and Character of William James*. Boston, Little and Brown.

Phillipson, M. (1989). *In Modernity's Wake: The Ameurunculus Letters*. London, Routledge.

Pike, K. L. (1967). *Live Issues in Descriptive Linguistics*. Santa Ana, Calif., Summer Institute of Linguistics.

Pinar, W. F. (1974). Self and others. Papers presented at the Xavier University Curriculum Theory Conference, Cincinnati.

Pinar, W. F. (1980). Life history and educational experience. *Journal of Curriculum Theorizing*, **2**, 159–212.

Pinar, W. F. (1981a). Life history and educational experience. *Journal of Curriculum Theorizing*, **3**, 259–86.

Pinar, W. F. (1981b). 'Whole, bright, deep with understanding': Issues in qualitative research and autobiographical method. *Journal of Curriculum Studies*, **13**, 173–88.

Plummer, K. (1983). *Documents of Life: An Introduction to the Problems and Literature of a Humanistic Method*. London, Allen & Unwin.

Polanyi, M. (1958). *Personal Knowledge: Toward a Post-Critical Philosophy*. Chicago, Ill., University of Chicago Press.

Pope, M. (1978). Monitoring and reflecting in teaching training. In F. Fransella (ed.), *Personal Construct Psychology 1977*, pp. 75–86. London, Academic Press.

Popkewitz, T. S., Tabachnick, R. B. and Zeichner, K. M. (1979). Dulling the senses: Research in teacher education. *Journal of Teacher Education*, **30**, 52–60.

Powell, J. P. (1985). The residues of learning: Autobiographical accounts by graduates of the impact of higher education. *Higher Education*, **14**, 127–47.

Radley, A. R. (1974). The effect of role enactment upon construed alternatives. *British Journal of Medical Psychology*, **47**, 313–20.

Rae, J. (1987). *Letters from School*. London, Collins.

Rank, O. (1936). *Truth and Reality*. New York, Knopf.

Raphael, F. (1976). *The Glittering Prizes*. Harmondsworth, Penguin.

Ravenette, A. T. (1988). A drawing and its opposite: An application of the notion of the 'construct' in the elaboration of children's drawings. Paper, Centre for Personal Construct Psychology, London.

Romanyshyn, R. D. (1982). *Psychological Life: From Science to Metaphor*. Milton Keynes, Open University Press.

Rosen, H. (1988). Struck by a particular gap. In M. Jones and A. West (eds), *Learning Me Your Language: Perspectives on the Teaching of English*, pp. 2–12. London, Mary Glasgow.

Rosenham, D. (1969). Some origins of concerns for others. In P. Mussen, J. Langer and M. Covington (eds), *Trends and Issues in Developmental Psychology*, pp. 134–53. New York, Holt.

Ryan, K., Applegate, J., Flora, V. R., Johnston, J., Lasley, T., Mager, G. and Newman, K. (1979). My teacher education program? *Peabody Journal of Education*, **56**, 267–71.

Sacks, O. (1985). *The Man Who Mistook His Wife for a Hat*. London, Picador.

Salmon, P. (1978). Doing psychological research. In F. Fransella (ed.), *Personal Construct Psychology 1977*, pp. 35–44. London, Academic Press.

Salmon, P. (1983). A personal approach to teaching psychology. In D. Pilgrim (ed.), *Psychology and Psychotherapy*, pp. 85–95. London, Routledge & Kegan Paul.

Salmon, P. (1985). *Living in Time: A New Look at Personal Development*. London, Dent.

Salmon, P. (1988). *Psychology for Teachers: An Alternative Approach*. London, Hutchinson.

Sartre, J.-P. (1964). *Words*. Harmondsworth, Penguin.

Sartre, J.-P. (1968). *Search for a Method*. New York, Random House.

Scholes, R. (1988). 'Three views of education: Nostalgia, history and voodoo. *College English*, **50**, 323–34.

Shaw, M. L. G. (1980). *On Becoming a Personal Scientist*. London, Academic Press.

Shulman, L. S. (1983). Autonomy and obligation. In L. S. Shulman and G. Sykes (eds), *Handbook of Teaching and Policy*, pp. 484–504. New York, Longman.

Simon, B. and Whitbread, N. (1988). A malign bill. *Forum*, **30**, 35.

Smyth, J. (1989a). A research agenda: An alternative vision. *Journal of Curriculum and Supervision*, **4**, 162–77

Smyth, J. (1989b). Developing and sustaining critical reflection in teacher education. *Journal of Teacher Education*, **40**, 2–9.

Stephens, R. (1985). *Personal Worlds*. Milton Keynes, Open University.

Stringer, P. (1985). You decide what your title is to be and (read) write to that title. In D. Bannister (ed.), *Issues and Prospects in Personal Construct Theory*, pp. 211–29. London, Academic Press.

Stringer, P. (1988). Fragmentation. In F. Fransella and L. F. Thomas (eds), *Experimenting with Personal Construct Psychology*, pp. 548–57. London, Routledge.

Tardif, C. (1985). On becoming a teacher: The student teacher's perspective. *Alberta Journal of Educational Research*, **31**, 139–48.

Terhart, E. (1982). Interpretative approaches in educational research: A consideration of some theoretical issues – with particular reference to recent developments in West Germany. *Cambridge Journal of Education*, **12**, 141–60.

Terkel, S. (1977). *Working*. Harmondsworth, Penguin.

Thomas, L. F. (1976). *Focusing: Exhibiting the Meanings in a Grid*. Uxbridge, Centre for the Study of Human Learning, Brunel University.

Thomas, L. F. (1979). Construct, reflect, converse. In P. Stringer and D. Bannister (eds), *Constructs of Sociality and Individuality*, pp. 49–71. London, Academic Press.

Thomas, L. F., McKnight, G. and Shaw, M. L. G. (1976). *Grids and Group Structure*. Uxbridge, Centre for the Study of Human Learning, Brunel University.

Thomas, W. I. and Znaniecki, F. (1958). *The Polish Peasant in Europe and America*. New York, Dover.

Thomson, A. (1985). Pupils as mirrors. *Forum*, **27**, 85–7.

Tiberius, R. (1980). Consulting to improve university teaching. *Options*, **7**, 4–6.

Traves, P. (1988). Ministering to their needs? An analysis of Kenneth Baker and George Walden on language and literature. In M. Jones and A. West (eds), *Learning Me Your Language: Perspectives on the Teaching of English*, pp. 171–84. London, Mary Glasgow.

Veenman, S. (1984). Perceived problems of beginning teachers. *Review of Educational Research*, **54**, 143–78.

Vygotsky, L. S. (1962). *Thought and Language*. Cambridge, Mass., MIT Press.

Vygotsky, L. S. (1979). *Mind in Society: The Development of Higher Psychological Processes*, M. Cole, V. John-Steiner, S. Scribner and E. Souberman (eds). Cambridge, Mass., Harvard University Press.

Vygotsky, L. S. (1981). The genesis of higher mental functions. In J. V. Wertsch (ed.), *The Concepts of Activity in Soviet Psychology*, pp. 144–88. New York, Sharpe.

White, R. W. (1975). *Lives in Progress*. New York, Holt.

Wildemeersch, D. and Leirman, W. (1988). The facilitation of the life-world transformation. *Adult Education Quarterly*, **39**, 19–30.

Woods, P. (1985). Conversations with teachers: Some aspects of life-history method. *British Educational Research Journal*, **11**, 13–25.

Yonemura, M. (1982). Teacher conversations: A potential source of their own professional growth. *Curriculum Inquiry*, **12**, 239–55.

Yorke, D. M. (1987). Construing classrooms and curricula: A framework for research. *British Educational Research Journal*, **13**, 35–50.

Zeichner, K. and Tabachnick, B. R. (1981). The development of teacher perspectives. *Journal of Education for Teaching*, **11**, 1–25.

Index